# Future Proof Your College

# Michael Heppell

Hadrian Publications

Hadrian Business Centre

Church Street

Haydon Bridge

Northumberland NE47 6JG

Tel: 08456 733336

Tel: +44 (0)1434 688555

Fax: +44 (0)1434 688666

Website: www.michaelheppell.com

First published in Great Britain in 2007.

© **Hadrian Publications, 2007**

ISBN 978-0-9555-731-1-8

British Library Cataloguing in Publication Data.

A CIP catalogue record for this book can be obtained from the British Library.

Printed and bound in Great Britain by Ashford Colour Press, Hampshire.

The Publisher's policy is to use paper manufactured from sustainable forests.

# Contents

# A message from Jerry Jarvis, Managing Director, Edexcel

When Edexcel was invited to get involved in a project focusing on the future of Further Education, we were delighted to accept.

In both the academic and the vocational arenas, education has changed dramatically in the last decade and faces further, radical change in the future. This book, while not necessarily reflecting the views of Edexcel, gives a brilliant insight into the exciting challenges and opportunities ahead for all involved in the sector.

As a forward-looking organisation, we believe the key to dealing with change successfully lies in listening to our customers and understanding your needs. By working together, we can rise to the new challenges ahead, make the most of the opportunities they offer, and deliver a relevant, recognised and rewarding learning experience to change the lives of learners for the better.

That's advancing learning, changing lives.

Enjoy the book.

Jerry Jarvis
Managing Director
Edexcel


*I would like to thank Edexcel for being the brilliant catalyst, which kick-started this venture.*

*Michael Heppell*

# Welcome to Future Proof Your College

I should point out at this early stage that I don't know the answer to 'How to Future Proof your College' but I do know a few things I would be doing now if I was, like you, primarily involved in the world of Further Education.

Future proofing can be seen as a type of insurance. The better the policy the more secure you feel. As with any insurance, you hope you won't ever have to use it but if you do, you'll want your money's worth. And given the risks involved with the future of FE it makes sense to have a good insurance policy.

There are lots of ways to future proof yourself and your college – we'll explore many in this book. As you read, you'll see some of the ideas actually contradict each other. Some you'll agree with and others you won't. That's because the premise of this book is opinion.

I've spent much of the summer of 2007 carrying out interviews with Principals, employers, educationalists and stakeholders in the world of Further Education. I asked most of them the same questions and never for one minute did I expect to get the same answers from them all – that would be dull. Instead, I listened to opinions and, as you know, opinions are only worth as much as the value you place upon them. Some were brilliant, others a little boring – I've included the interviews, with minimal edits, as a major part of this book. So who's brilliant and who's boring? You decide.

My goal was to ensure each interview could be read in a few minutes and that each would be followed by a few hints and tips for future proofing.

Trust me – the future's fun.

# Why future proof?

Here's a flashback for you. Betamax or VHS? When I was a kid my Dad bought a VHS machine but he did consider Betamax. Phew, that was a close one. He could have future-proofed himself in several ways:

**1)** Not bought one. Waited until the battle was over and gone with the winner. This has the obvious upside of not being caught out, but the downside is the 2 year wait without a video recorder!

**2)** Bought both. He'd have been covered for every eventuality. A friend of mine did this with DVD's and Laser Discs in the 90's – but he had more money than sense. That's the main downside of trying to cover all your options. Yes there's the money but we just don't have enough time to think of every option.

**3)** Get good advice. By spending some time talking to knowledgeable people, reading, researching and weighing up the pro's and con's you can make an informed choice.

Luckily, my Dad went for Option 3. Mind you, no-one told him how many hours it would take out of his already busy life to learn how to programme the new machine!

Most people associate future proofing with IT. No one wants to be caught out investing thousands of pounds in a system only to find it won't integrate with the latest software, networks and features. This book will give you about 1% of the expert knowledge you'll need for that area of future proofing. If you need to know more about future proofing IT, get on-line, there are over a million pages on the subject. This is about future proofing the heart of Further Education, the staff, the environment, the learning, the experience and most importantly the students.

If you spend some time future proofing now, your payback will be a hundred fold in the future – the near future.

*"We should all be concerned about the future because we will have to spend the rest of our lives there."*

**Charles F. Kettering**

# How it works

You'll see this book consists of several main styles. They are:

**Interviews** I took a selection of people and interviewed them asking the same basic questions. All interviewees gave their time for free and signed off their interviews before publication.

**Rants!** A rant is where I asked some people to let off steam. The deal was I would edit them but not reveal who wrote them.

**Tests, teasers and quizzes** A bit of fun but also an opportunity to see how future savvy you are and to encourage debate.

**Learning** I'm a professional speaker and trainer. I spend most of my life working with organisations large and small, teaching them 'How to be Brilliant' and how to create amazing customer service experiences. I've added some of my teachings to help you prepare for the future.

**Quotes** I love motivational quotes. You'll find them peppered throughout this book. When you read one, ask yourself 'What does this mean to me?' before moving on.

# 1

# Interview
## with Dame Ruth
## Silver
### Lewisham College

# Interview with Dame Ruth Silver DBE, Principal and Chief Executive, Lewisham College

*Ruth has worked in senior management in Further Education for fifteen years and is currently Principal of Lewisham College, London. She holds a number of national posts linked to learning in Further Education, has written and broadcasted extensively on educational matters and is committed to Inclusiveness, particularly in the inner city.*

**MH** What are you doing right now to Future Proof your College?

**RS** Gosh everything I can! The first thing we've done is to navigate our way towards the new agenda, which is of course: demand-led, skills and personalisation. So tackling the three dimensions – the triangulation of change! Demand-led is not the same as the skills agenda.

We have produced a new Strategic Plan, which is called 'Achieving Ambitions' in which we lay out the 5 platforms for change. They are:

Personalisation of learning
Professionalisation of staff
Partnerships of purpose
Procurement of opportunities and purses
Place – taking and making a 'place' for this College in the new region that's London

**MH** The 5- P's – fantastic!

**RS** Simplicity comes in useful, doesn't it! We have now printed and told the story of what we'll become. It's our College framework for change really.

**MH** And what sort of timescale are you looking at?

**RS** It's a five year intention but it's really three years operationally. We're a double Beacon College and we're here in the Thames gateway with the Mayor of London's new Skills and Employment Board so it's very different in London. We have put the story-board there, the script is there, colleagues here know what they are authorised to do at Lewisham College and they now have the authority to go and help that happen.

The plan is strongly endorsed by Governors and staff. The main thing we've done is we have re-engineered the College to 'beef up' the Business Development units. So we have moved from two/three years ago from having 4 people doing it, to currently having 14, and in September we'll have 24 new colleagues.

We have brought all our schools and delivery schools under one lead person – a Vice Principal of Skills – and we are putting Business Development in there with him. We held this under a separate manager while we found the range, pace and skill of it. We are now starting the next phase of the systemic cultural change, which is that the business developers will help our traditional FE people learn to be different.

**MH** What does that mean, 'learn to be different?'

**RS** In order to get changed behaviours in an organisation, you have to describe the behaviours you're looking for. So we've begun. Take 'Business Development'; if I caricature this, the skills they have in sales are really about relationship and account management; and the skills of our teachers and their managers are about 'student centredness', curriculum development, teaching and learning. There now needs to be a mutation.

**MH** In terms of when you get to that point in five years time, who do you think your most important customers will be?

**RS** One minute, it's a three year plan not a five year and our most important customers will be exactly the ones they are now – the learners!

They may not be here in College; they probably won't be in the organisation; so if we can satisfy the learner, the feedback to their employer will be about how well the College has served them – terrific.

So it's about the chain reaction really – that learners will always, always be delighted about the learning undertaken at Lewisham College

**MH** Fantastic. It sounds like you have some major plans. How will you fund what you want to do in the future?

**RS** By winning – on the basis of specialising in success – the contracts, the commissions that are the ways of the new world! We also have a Development Fund in the College. We run a culture of 'project bagging' so the college has about 30 projects at the moment. All projects at Lewisham College are seen as a 'rehearsal studio for the future', so we have been funded by the Beacon Unit to develop a Personalisation Project this year. We have been funded by the Edge Foundation to design teacher training in Practical Learning. We've been funded by the LSC to look at a partnership with two other colleges.

**MH** So would you say the money is out there but you have to create the exciting projects to attract the funding?

**RS** It's all part of the navigation – to map your objective towards their objective so that it fits and it's all in one.

**MH** Brilliant! What mistakes do you want to avoid making in the next few years?

**RS** Goodness me..., taking the easy way out, putting all my eggs in one basket, reducing sight of learning, undernourishing the teachers.

**MH** Speaking of teachers, what do you think the ideal future teaching staff are going to look like?

**RS** We have just designed, funded by Edge, through London's South Bank University a new qualification in 'Teaching of Practical Learning'.

So that's what we're looking for; it's teachers who can teach their skills. You'll know this. We used to send our plumbing teachers, dance teachers and beauty therapy teachers to learn to be teachers/trainers at university and they followed a very academic curriculum – the Politics, History and Sociology of Education. They have to write essays, they have to do things that actually de-skill them rather than endorse and expand the skills they have in the first place.

So that's the most important part for me – it's how we take their professional skills and absolutely shore these up while introducing ways of teaching it to other people. That's crucial. We need people who know about blended learning, who know about functional skills. We need colleagues who can handle their worlds, who know about relationship management, who are proud of both their original profession and their new one that is teaching it to others – skilfully.

**MH** What about your ideal support staff in the future?

**RS** Well we've introduced here a foundation degree in 'Education Administration' for our support staff. All of them – and us – will have to be systems literate and know about compliance. They will have to be absolutely terrific customer service people and they have to see and ensure that the teaching, management structure and quality of colleague internal customers matter as much as an external customer.

It's the same for teaching staff – relationship management. Where we have an agenda that we wish to put through, such as 'Achieving Ambitions' (our plan) it has learning and development underpinning – CPD – from staff. In fact it's our fourth plan. Our first was called 'Constructing Capabilities', our second 'Promising Prospects' and our third, 'Pushing Prosperity'. Achieving Ambitions has got three strands: teaching people about their roles and their responsibilities at Lewisham College; the routine of Lewisham College; and their relationship management skills.

**MH** So really you are saying that the most important learners are your own people first?

**RS** Oh absolutely, absolutely!

**MH** Who do you see as your future partners?

**RS** Learners. Given personalisation in the agenda, learners are key partners in the College's ambition; employers are key; local schools and communities.

**MH** How do you get employers as excited about education as you are?

**RS** Well that is the challenge for all in this system. This is a fabulous agenda and employers have been given the honourable lead in it all. The question remains though, will employers pick up this fabulous position the Government has given them? I certainly hope so. My experience here gives me confidence too.

We have a Business Breakfast Club that meets once a month, where employers meet with us and each other and we seek ways of supporting local prosperity. We have a large and successful employers' award ceremony. We have a great deal of ongoing contact with them, lots of marketing with them. And we are now under a very strategic steer from the Employer's Council at Lewisham College.

'Train to Gain' has been both strenuous and terrific for helping us rehearse the future in the hands of our Business Development Group. We're re-engineering the College, more and more moving students and colleagues on and up into the skills agenda. We have developed e-learning facilities so that people can access learning on-line. We have a large Trade Union study centre so we reach the workplace through that portal as well.

**MH** So tell me of the role of the future Principal. If you're future proofing yourself, what are you doing?

**RS** The key to learning is skilful relationship management, particularly the skills required in partnerships. I don't know what you've learned about life but my experience is that actually leadership is easy – it's co-leadership that's incredibly complicated.

It's that sense of needing good communication skills in a partnership, that kind of building of resilience… how to handle difficulties. To learn how to give up things in order to find new things – I think that is key.

The Principal of the future will have to be able to do two things at the same time; be an expert on learning and an expert on selling.

**MH** I know that you love Lewisham but if you had the opportunity to open a new college now, what are the three things that you would focus on first?

**RS** I would focus on a future, fitting concept, taking that round and talking. I would wish to undertake a communication engagement campaign, to win hearts – and purses – for the new institution.

I would focus on how to have that endorsed – working on that with staff as well as recruiting the staff themselves.

I'd focus on the learning environment and I'm not just talking about a building, I'm talking about the ICT infrastructure and the intelligent way of running a new organisation.

**MH** Are there any questions that you wished I'd asked you?

**RS** Something about 'What's the political decorum that future Principals need'

Geoff Stanton, a very wise teacher, said to me, 'the struggle with the English education system is that colleagues are terrific with their subject and they are terrific with their students but they're not good at seeing the wider system they work within'. So much of the rumble you get is because people don't clarify that they are public servants in the independent college sector. This isn't helped by the focus on public value when in our world, we are more concerned with social and economic value.

One of the key skills of the future Principal is that of political literacy. And that's with a big P *and* a small p, Michael.

*"The Principal of the future will have to be able to do two things at the same time; be an expert on learning and an expert on selling."*

**Dame Ruth Silver DBE**

# 2

# Risk it for a biscuit

# Risk it for a biscuit

When I was at school we would often challenge each other to 'risk it for a biscuit'. I don't think I ever got the biscuits but I was always one for taking a risk.

Nowadays the risk and reward ratio is much greater; the rules more complicated and the number of people at stake much higher. But taking risk now to benefit you and your organisation in the future has never been more important.

The hardest part of taking a risk is making your mind up. Once the decision is made it's relatively easy to deal with the consequences. Making our mind up is one of the hardest things – or is it?

I'll bet you, like me, have made some of the biggest decisions of your life in a heartbeat. Just think; we are where we are now because of some, often split second decisions we made years ago.

I'm not suggesting you should be fearful of making decisions, I want to bring the idea of 'decision making' to the forefront of your mind.

During a speech, Chris Patton, the former Governor of Hong Kong, mentioned that one of the things he most admired in great leaders was their ability to make decisions – and stick with them. With this in mind I've put together my:

**Five steps to brilliant decision making**

**1)** Trust your intuition. Your intuition is always right. Yet how many times have you found yourself saying, 'I wish I'd listened to that 'hunch', or in an exasperated way shouted, 'I knew it!'

**2)** Make decisions based on your values. If you have a strong values system it's easier to make decisions as they are based on core beliefs rather than external forces or whims.

**3)** Appoint internal advisors. If you're going to have a 'voice in your head', choose a person whose advice you would trust. It doesn't mean you're crazy if you 'talk to' an imaginary advisor – it's just another way of tapping in to your deeper intuition.

**4)** Use Edison's Pad. The great inventor Thomas Edison would sleep with a pad and pencil next to his bed. At night he would write at the top of the page;

'while I am asleep I will wake up with the answer to...' He used this method frequently to maximise his subconscious brain power while he was sleeping. He woke up knowing the answer.

5) Finally, here's a great quote from Yogi Berra, 'When you reach a fork in the road, take it'. Ok, so that's not the best advice ever, but dig a little deeper and you'll see that often people don't make any decision for fear they make the wrong decision.

My advice? Act on the above and go for it – even if you take the wrong fork at least you'll be on the journey rather than standing still, scratching your head and wondering!

*"Your destiny is made during moments of decision."*

**Tony Robbins**

# 3

# Interview with Rosie Du Rose 02 Ltd

# Interview with Rosemary Du Rose, General Manager, O2 Ltd

*Rosemary has spent the majority of her career managing large customer service centres in the financial services and telecoms industries. At O2 she is the General Manager for Transformational Change and has accountability for delivering strategies to deliver exceptional customer and people experience whilst delivering improvements to stakeholder's value.*

**MH** What are your expectations from a learning provider and how can you see that changing in the next five years?

**RDR** I want a learning provider to know my business and understand exactly what it is we do and how they can support that. With this in mind I need them to be able to essentially provide me with a range of business/learning solutions. I currently believe that too many current day solutions are "off the shelf" and do not fully meet my requirements. Helping me to understand possibilities and options/variants would allow me to consider alternative approaches.

I would also like that provider or college to be able to add value to my team or training personnel so that I am not totally dependent on that learning provider for any length of time. I want to be able to grow that skill, knowledge and aptitude within my business.

I want them to be able to offer a blended approach. I expect them to be knowledgeable and understanding of what is current thinking and best practice.

They would also inform me of potential trends and developments in relation to key development needs that impact my business e.g. technology

I think all too often we "stick with what we know" and just tweak current practice rather than embrace radical thinking and new innovation.

**MH** And what about in five years time?

**RDR** I think the world is changing and particularly in telecoms. I need solutions and I need them quick! Leading and managing large organisations and contact centres mean that training solutions and information needs to be provided in an efficient and engaging way. In addition, it needs to support the relevant learning styles of the individual and encourage the individual to take the initiative in respect of their own self-development.

In summary, flexible, fast and relevant. In addition, I would like to be able to truly measure, in all instances, the return on investment; I think we continue to struggle to be definitive when it comes to ROI for L&D activity.

**MH** Is that to actually show you what sort of impact it's going to have on bottom line?

**RDR** Yes, how do you truly understand that impact? In addition, we probably need to tie providers into more risk and reward aspects of any contracts so that they truly have a stake in the delivery of any benefits.

**MH** Do you have partnerships with colleges at the moment?

**RDR** A few – particularly where we have apprenticeship schemes in place.

**MH** If a college was to come to you and say – 'we'll be able to train your staff and get them to a point where you could put them straight on to the telephones', would that excite you?

**RDR** Yes it would! Then they would need to convince me how they planned to do it and provide credible results

**MH** Because your own training system is so well developed in terms of what you do to get people to that stage?

**RDR** No, I wouldn't say that at all – we have more to do and always will have! I think they would have to convince me that they have best practice and would deliver additional value. It is possible – I've just yet to see such a scheme truly delivering that level of capability. Contact Centre work is not low skilled – it requires a high degree of social, people and conversational capability coupled with the right attitude and ability to assimilate knowledge and solve problems quickly. Add to that the particular dynamics and nature of the actual business and it adds up to a significant challenge.

**MH** I've heard so many employers' views on a typical situation where a prospective employee arrives with a piece of paper which says 'I have a qualification in....' but is not actually 'fit for purpose' in the workplace.

**RDR** I think most training via colleges is based around teaching the technical and system capability – e.g. teaching people how to use PC's and knowledge base systems. Whilst this supports Customer Service skill, it is not teaching the customer experience, insight and conversational aspects.

**MH** How do you know when a learner has been successful? What are your measurements for that?

**RDR** We assess them – once at the end of the training module(s) and then on an on-going basis through performance management and coaching. If a learning intervention/training takes place we are expecting some element of the individual's performance to improve.

**MH** So you're looking for a permanent behavioural shift?

**RDR** Yes

**MH** When it comes to buying training – and you obviously invest a lot in that – how do you gauge best value?

**RDR** We want people to understand, or show that they have a good understanding of our business, customer and people strategies, so that they can clearly demonstrate that they're providing us with solutions which are aligned to those strategies.

Best value is also a provider who future proofs any solutions e.g. how can the transfer of such skills be made to my own team and how can I maintain the knowledge/information. For instance, if they're offering me a CBT package, we as an organisation can subsequently revise, adapt and update without any additional cost.

Too many times in the past I've been provided with supposedly 'leading edge', only to find myself having to pay huge fees to make what have been seemingly minor changes. I need suppliers/providers to want to be partners and commit to my business for the medium to longer term.

A true partnership, making sure that all the solutions they give me are beneficial to both of us.

**MH** What mistakes do you think FE makes that you wish they didn't?

**RDR** I think there needs to be a balance, more of a swing to vocational rather than academic. In areas where there are major social, educational and economic requirements it is imperative that we have a balance towards the vocational as much as the academic.

I think the academic element is great, if people can then translate that into 'what do I do now? How does this get me a job or career or how does this actually place me into society and utilise those skills'. I don't necessarily think the academic element truly meets this need.

I want it to be more pragmatic, more practical and if it means swinging the pendulum towards a more vocational approach then that's what we should do.

**MH** Imagine I'm going to give you a new job. You are now the Principal of a brand new FE college. What three things would you focus on first?

**RDR** I would understand the community that that college was in and the businesses that needed to be supported. I am curious as to what we need to do as a business to forge stronger and more appropriate relationships.

I think I'd make sure that I was able to prove in some way, shape or form (I don't know what that is) that what the college was providing could be evaluated in a way that the community would see that there was a definite change as a result of that FE establishment being there.

School leavers would have a number of options from the vocational to the academic and high profile apprenticeship schemes that were valued.

E.g. if my child at 16 was going into an apprenticeship scheme with O2, that I, as a parent, would know that it was considered to be a great achievement and that they got on it. That they're going to work for O2 and they are a great employer.

I would want colleges to support businesses from that perspective rather than saying, 'you don't want to end up in a Call Centre!'

**MH** You've seen a huge amount of teaching and training of staff in your time. What would you like future teaching staff to look like?

**RDR** I think there would be the balance between business, vocational and academic. I'm a great believer in people achieving and I think there are different ways that people achieve and at the moment we could do more to recognise and nurture true talent and skills – whatever they may be.

In Call Centres, people come to us from all walks of life including the textile industry, where they have been in roles which have been low skilled work and poorly paid. We value their attitude, give them new skills and confidence and they then tell us 'that's the first time somebody's told me I'm good at something'.

I need people to be enthusiastic and motivated and I almost want to see them understand the importance of what they contribute to the business and their community overall.

I want them to be committed to achieving results. For me, that's not just about the number of A-grade students – it's about improving employment prospects across the spectrum and recognising that there is value in all work as well as in going to college and university.

*"I need solutions and I need them quick!"*

**Rosemary Du Rose, O2 Ltd**

# 4

# Mind the gap!

## Mind the gap!

| How it was | How it is | How it will be |
|---|---|---|
| Know your place | Raise your game | Lead or die |
| Not my job | Know who to call | Be the expert |
| Job for life | Career opportunity | Performance for now |
| Get away with it | Do a good job | Brilliance is the benchmark |
| Departments | Whole approach | Funky teams |
| Moan and be heard | Moan and be by-passed | Be 'up for it' or get out |
| Tied down | Know the ropes | Bungee! |
| Follow the curriculum | Adapt for learners | Create everything |
| Uncomfortable with change | Acclimatised | Designed flexibility |
| Us and them | Partnership | Integration |
| Follow the rules | Break the rules | No rules |
| Own a PC | Get linked | Global multi device real-time connectivity |
| Wait until we're asked | Cold calls | Integrated into every opportunity |
| Need it whenever | Need it asap | Anticipate – I needed it yesterday |

*"Disconnecting from change does not recapture the past. It loses the future."*

**Kathleen Norris, O Magazine, January 2004**

# 5

# Interview with Andy Cole

## Dollond & Aitchison

# Interview with Andy Cole, HR Director, Dollond & Aitchison

*Andy leads the D&A Academy, responsible for clinical and retail training, management learning and the development of senior business and professional colleagues. The Academy provides nearly 4000 training days a year for Optometrists, Managers and Retail Advisers.*

**MH** What are your expectations from a learning provider right now, and how can you see that changing in the next five years?

**AC** Is that more about having the qualifying people to come into work? Are you describing a learning provider in that way?

**MH** Or any type of learning provider – what are you looking for?

**AC** What I want from a learning provider is that they have an understanding of my business, a developed understanding of my business and have credibility in terms of learning, design and they aren't selling me a tried old process. They are genuinely offering me something that will help individuals learn rather than – here's our philosophy, here's our process, follow these six steps and everything's fine. It needs to be more and more of a relationship, I think.

**MH** Obviously your business is rapidly changing. How do you think that learning providers are going to need to change for you in the next five years?

**AC** I think that in our marketplace now, the whole thing around the skills agenda – everybody having to achieve Level 2, everybody having good numeracy and literacy and other Leitch emphasis on beyond Level 4 qualifications to remain competitive – I think that would be something the learning providers should be involved with, understanding the Government skills agenda because I don't think it will change whatever colour of government we have, that idea about competitive advantage is very much there.

**MH** Do you partner with particular colleges at the moment?

**AC** No, because we are our own college. We provide a City & Guilds qualification, Level 2 and 3.

**MH** Where does that take place?

**AC** It takes place here in Birmingham for the core elements then work-based learning with effectively NVQ assessors, all of whom are employed by the business. They all have other roles so most of our NVQ assessors are Branch Managers or Dispensing Opticians with a commitment to help their newer colleagues learn.

**MH** Why do you do that in-house rather than sub-contracting it out to the colleges?

**AC** Primarily because we're quite a specialist retailer, so I don't think that those skills are in the marketplace or in the Further Education sector anyway and the other reason is surely because we are more efficient at it. It's all work-based learning so everything we do, (apart from the training time we provide centrally which is still a working day), we gain efficiency in time. So I don't have to send my people to college – they don't have to do it in their own time – I'm not talking about day release or anything like that – it's all provided through work. We also had a stake in writing the qualification within our sector.

**MH** How would you gauge the success of a learner?

**AC** In terms of our NVQ provision, they've all got jobs – so we just make it mandatory to train them. I think it's impact on behaviour. I may need Levels 2 to 4 in terms of learning, I also want a return on the investment and we would track that ultimately through what our customer says. We're a business that builds itself on recommendations really, so alongside our mystery shopping, our customer service surveys are absolutely key.

**MH** Do you buy any training in at the moment from external providers?

**AC** I do but not a great deal. I'm blessed to have a very skilful team and the majority of what we do is in-house. I have two partnerships – one with Aston Business School – who run elements of an MBA programme for our Senior Managers – and a company called Red Sky Learning who do a sort of level 4 Management qualification. So for my Senior Management, I have partnerships with those providers but that would be it – so that's around 10%.

**MH** How do you gauge best value when you're buying in that training?

**AC** I simply use my experience of the market. I just know. I've been on the consultancy side as well for a long time.

**MH** Never knock intuition. Even when it's wrong, it's right. What mistakes do you think FE makes at the moment, which you wish they didn't?

**AC** I suppose my experience of them is that they're institutions. I don't understand what benefit they would provide to me locally, so I don't know. The way they are represented to me in my role in this company is through the Learning & Skills Council; through Train to Gain initiatives so I have an impression, which is, they are a big anonymous body.

There is massive benefit in them providing people with good literacy and good numeracy, good problem solving, good communication skills and being good at customer service. If I had those colleges providing me with those levels of qualifications, I could probably make the technical elements fit but nobody is talking to me about that. I'm not saying that I would absolutely do it, but nobody is pitching to me in a way that other private sector providers would do.

Apart from possibly the Open University – I don't know whether you see them as Further Education. They have quite a good corporate arm, which makes sense.

**MH** Imagine you're going to set up your own college – what three things would you focus on?

**AC** I would focus on: team working, communication and (if I could combine the two) literacy and numeracy – the functional skills.

**MH** What type of staff would you be looking to recruit?

**AC** Simple – people from business.

*"The consequences of our actions are so complicated, so diverse, that predicting the future is a very difficult business indeed."*

*J. K. Rowling,*
*Harry Potter and the Prisoner of Azkaban*

# 6

**One** chance
to make a **first**
**impression**

# One chance to make a first impression

When I was a fundraiser in the 1990's I was responsible for raising money from schools and colleges. After being in the job for two years, I could pretty much go in to a meeting and know within ten minutes exactly how much money they would raise. I was usually right within £50. The first impression given by any organisation is generally a reflection of the entire organisation.

I could tell how well a school would do by the ease with which I found the entrance. I knew how well a college would do by the state of the car park and the greeting at reception.

In the last 12 months I've visited over 30 FE colleges in the UK and several overseas. We've had every type of welcome from, 'you can't park there', to the incredible 'first impression' from Lesley at Salisbury College, who greets guests as if they are arriving at a five star hotel. I'd like to think I'm easy going and I don't get upset by poor first impressions, but who am I kidding?

The college of the future will ensure every customer touch point is world class because the customer of the future won't stand for anything less.

# Rant!

If the car parking places closest to the entrance are reserved for senior staff you're heading for trouble. No one wants to do business with an organisation where you have to park half a mile away while the senior team are 'all right Jack'.

*"The future, according to some scientists, will be exactly like the past, only far more expensive."*

**John Sladek**

# 7

## Interview with Brian Turtle

### Belfast Metropolitan College

# Interview with Brian Turtle CBE, Director and Chief Executive, Belfast Metropolitan College

*Brian has worked in the Education Sector for 35 years, 11 of which he has been Chief Executive of a series of colleges. For the last 5 years he has been Director and Chief Executive of the Belfast Institute which merged in 2007 with Castlereagh College to form the Belfast Metropolitan College.*

**MH** What are you doing right now to Future Proof your College?

**BT** We believe we need a constituency and that constituency has to be the world of employment. To date, the link between employment, employers and employees is the job ad in the newspaper. We believe the link should be the college so we are working very closely with employers defining specific needs and specific provision that will lead to the employment of students. We are then offering that provision to students and the result is more motivation and more people understanding the value of what we do.

**MH** Can you give me an example of where you've done that with somebody already?

**BT** Yes – we've a number of major employers coming to Northern Ireland. One would be Citigroup. What we're doing there is that they've specified a particular course that they want, including validation from the Stock Exchange, and they've indicated how they would like it delivered. We're now creating 600 workers for them but these workers are maybe people who would have come on courses in the past without the prospect of specific employment. We can now create a focus and explain to people that if they follow this provision, there will be jobs at a particular salary level and so what we're really doing is enhancing the relevance of what we do.

We're also doing this with other organisations such as IKEA, House of Fraser and a whole series of construction businesses and engineering companies like Bombardier. It's a style of approach where, instead of us just teaching people and then them falling into a chasm where employers find them, we're really helping people understand that if they study in this particular provision it's taking them in the direction of their employment aspirations.

We are also trying to back that into schools by saying to schools if they were taking some link provision/vocational enhancement provision, they can engage with us on a similar basis and that the employment escalator can start at the age of 14.

**MH** Wow – that sounds very exciting. It almost sounds as though you're putting the cart before the horse but actually at the moment the cart is before the horse and you're just putting the horse in the right place.

**BT** People have always said that FE is supply-driven, that we pick the courses studied. In reality, the people who choose courses in Belfast are the students and sometimes those choices are not well grounded in reality, as their understanding of the labour market is limited. Why would you expect a 16 year old to understand the labour market? What we're trying to do is be a bit more proactive. The result of it is employers are viewing us as more important to them. It also means that agencies such as Invest Northern Ireland (our Government agency responsible for inward investment) are coming to us to speak to employers and bringing us in and acting out of their resources, paying for CPD work in companies because suddenly what they see is our provision being relevant to dealing with a skills problem. But the strategic thinking of it all is that we now have a constituency. People in various Government departments and employers have come to realise that we have a greater value and relevance rather than us being just a College providing education and training which is supply driven.

Primary schools would rely on parents; if somebody was threatening a primary school or reducing its budget then parents would be very upset about it. Here, I'm not sure that's the constituency – we think a key constituency are the employers and the whole support structure in the UK for economic development – which is sort of a major theme in Government. We're placing ourselves as significant deliverers in that field.

**MH** Who do you think your most important customer is going to be in five years time?

**BT** Our most important customers are always our students but at the same time what I'm saying is that the students know that if they come here, what they'll be doing will be relevant to improvements in their salary and their employability. And to some extent the background customers (the employers) know that we are using our knowledge of local needs now to influence the students. But the students are still massively the customer.

We're also future proofing ourselves by providing a massive amount of support for the students using virtual learning; that's a whole area of our activity where we are endeavouring to make sure that students, when they are not in the classroom, still have a way of learning and having that learning validated.

**MH** Do you think that a future student of yours, in five or 10 years time, mightn't need to come to one of your buildings?

**BT** No – we believe in blended learning. We believe that it's important socially that learners need to have the confidence of the support of the lecturer but what we're saying is that that can be added to; particularly if they're part time students. For example, through protected discussion groups where students who, when they're out of class, allow learners to still be working on projects together that can be monitored by staff and staff can have an input giving direction.

We also believe, particularly for our Higher Education students, that it's important that when they leave us they don't just have a qualification. We are giving them 6 weeks working on industry-sponsored projects either in a business or in cross-curricular groups within the College, so that they leave with a CV in addition to their qualifications. They've worked on a project; they've designed, for example, a waste management policy for a local restaurant. They will have worked on a project that they can put on a CV. Our challenge is that more and more employers want experienced people now. We create people with qualifications and skills and knowledge but now engagement with business is part of their time with us. This means they leave with a qualification, CV and the skills needed by employers gained through the project work. It also allows them to leave with a CV and a relationship with a local business.

**MH** ...and answers that statement, 'Well you have a qualification but you have no experience'

**BT** It means they have 6 weeks where an employer will reference their good work. We also think it's better learning. It's not all just theory – we're giving them an opportunity and we're assessing this process. 'If you're working on that project – what did you learn? Now let's validate that.' We think that's important.

**MH** How are you going to fund your future plans?

**BT** Well, to date what has happened is that our numbers have been growing on the back of this enhanced relevance. We also believe the use of technology makes the provision even more efficient. We believe that through this development of a more relevant curriculum and an understanding that if you come to us to improve your employability, we will create sustainability. We believe also the use of virtual learning will help the efficiency.

**MH** So it's almost like success breeds success.

**BT** That's it. I think at the end of the day we need to deliver the work more efficiently and the virtual learning helps that but we also need to make sure that students in a situation of demographic downturn see us as a preferred option.

**MH** What mistakes do you want to avoid making in the next five to ten years?

**BT** I think again there has been a long history, certainly in Northern Ireland of 'growth is king'. We think quality and relevance are king; so while sometimes we are happy that there are more students giving us greater market share, at the same time, we believe that we need to make sure that the quality of experience – more specifically the quality of relevant experience – will win the day. That will create a sustainable future.

We also believe that we need to change some of the models by which we teach people. That will require staff development and we need to make sure that staff development moves at a pace with the rest of the process.

We do need to make sure that our communication with students is effective because they need to understand what we're trying to do and how what we're doing is a better option than what they may get from, say, schools or in private training.

**MH** Of course. On the subject of staff, what do you think your future staff are going to be like?

**BT** They're going to be doing the sorts of things that they're doing today but I believe they'll also be managing project work and assessing people while they're engaged in the project work. They'll be using the virtual learning environment more and more to supplement class learning and one of the things we'll be having to do – in fact we are doing – is responding more flexibly in adjusting the curriculum to proactively meet the needs for local employability.

**MH** And what about your support staff – what will they be doing?

**BT** Again, we will have people supporting students in that project work. We will have people who are engaged in establishing a solid, ongoing relationship with employers. We've formed a service called Job Club, where employers can get lists of people with specific skills to meet their employment needs, to interview from us without having to go to the press.

**MH** Who do you see as your future partners to make these visions happen?

**BT** We've established an employer's forum for Belfast so we have representatives of all the main employers. We are very close to Sector Skills Councils, we're very close to the Local Authority in Belfast and of course there are a whole range of Government departments. We're working very closely with those departments involved in economic development, investment and in particular our own Department of Employment Learning.

**MH** Now what about your job – the role of the future Principal. How do think that's going to look?

**BT** It all depends on what you see as the role of the Principal. There are lots of roles for the Principal. My emphasis would be on trying to motivate people and establishing a system of values and objectives and communicating these through the organisation to achieve ownership. Clearly we are also Accounting Officers so we have to make sure we have a clear picture of the use of resources and how efficiently and effectively we are operating. But I think the Principal, bottom line, has to help staff understand why the vision is the vision and their role in its achievement. I actually think more and more that the Principal will become a coach of a top management team.

It's to ensure all of the staff understand the reason for the targets, and then buy into them, and also to help establish and deliver a set of values for the organisation. What we're here for can be summed up in 'building careers and enriching lives' and at the end of the day we need to make sure that that's what we're doing. On occasions, it's easy to get carried away on projects but the bottom line is we have to check all of what we're trying to do against those values. I think one of my key roles is to try and keep people to that.

**MH** If you had to start all over again, with a greenfield site, what are the three things you would focus on first?

**BT** I suppose the key thing would be to create roles or managers, teachers and support staff that facilitate the delivery of learning along the lines of that curriculum relevance to employability. We need to establish clear leadership roles at all levels and ensure these leaders have the training and support to lead and manage.

We actually have the opportunity to design accommodation which is fit for purpose in a major 20,000 sq metre development so we need to look at how the accommodation would facilitate learning. We have actually, within our new structure, put the estate's function within student services because we think the quality, accommodation, furniture and fittings is all part of the service to students. So we need to make sure that the accommodation that we have fits with staff and student needs.

We also need delivery/support staff models which allow us to create roles for people which are fit for what we're trying to do.

I think the other message right from the start is to brand the College as the place where people who have developed their general skills and knowledge at school, become able to make clear career choices and to attain better levels of employment because they've been educated and trained by us. To do that, we need to have established a new relationship with all the local business sectors.

*"The past is to be respected and acknowledged, but not to be worshipped. It is our future in which we will find our greatness."*

**Pierre Trudeau**

# 8

## How to be

## brilliant

# How to be brilliant

Here's an extract taken from my book *How To Be Brilliant* published by Pearson, Prentice Hall. If there was ever a model to help you to Future Proof, then this is it.

## Time to be brilliant

When Sydney won the bid to host the Olympics for the Year 2000 it was an exciting time for Australia. I was fortunate to be introduced to the guy who was the Sydney Olympics Lighting Director and so I asked him about the Opening Ceremony. I don't know if you had a chance to see the Opening Ceremony but it was the most spectacular event I have ever witnessed. They had more colour, more excitement, more passion, more visual effects, more sound effects, better lighting and better fireworks. Everything was produced to the highest degree – it all came together amazingly tastefully – it worked so well.

I asked him how they planned an event like that and what it was that made such a difference. He said, "Michael, it started five years before the event, the creative team came together. The Chief Executive of The Sydney Olympics, Sandy Holloway walked into the room. He looked at us and he said, 'this is the brief for the Opening Ceremony of the 2000 Olympics. I would like you to get footage of every Olympics there has ever been. I would like you to obtain videos; to find books; acquire photographs, I would like you to unearth old audios; interview people; find out what was it that made these previous events as exciting as they were. Then I want you to take the very best, the most exciting, the most emotive and the most passionate parts of each event. Then bring all of that information together. Increase it to the power of 10 and that is your starting point!'

My new friend concluded, "Michael, we sat there with the hairs on the back of our necks standing on end. We knew we were about to create history. We knew that we were going to do something which had never been done before. We were so excited. For the next five years the excitement was just building all the time. We had to invent new technology to support our ideas. We wanted to do things that had never been done before and because of that excitement, passion and leadership, we were able to create an Opening Ceremony which has never been seen before. Not only that, but the whole Olympics continued to follow that same theme. We had the best transport system, it was the most organised Olympics for the athletes and the press, it was the cleanest, it had the best quality

– everybody agreed that Sydney stepped up and created something which was truly brilliant".

Why did it happen? How did it happen? Think about it! The days of doing a good job and expecting to get good results are long gone. It is no longer good enough to just be 'good'.

I often start presentations with, "I've done my research about you and there's good news and bad news. The good news is you're good." The delegates will usually cheer at that point, but then I continue with, 'the bad news is... you're good!'

Here's how Brilliance Benchmarking works. Imagine a race is about to begin – we'll stick with an Olympic theme and make it the Men's Olympic 100m. How much faster does the winner have to be than the second placed runner to take the gold medal? In Athens 2004 the difference between first, second and third was one hundredth of a second.

What sort of difference did that make to the first three in the minutes, hours, days and months which followed? Well, the winner gets a gold medal. Oh and millions of dollars in sponsorship, then there's the opportunity to work with the best trainers and have the best equipment and not forgetting the prospect of being able to run in any race meeting anywhere in the world – everyone wants the Olympic champion.

Take a moment to think about the ones who came second and third. They missed out on a gold medal and all those rewards by one hundredth of a second. They spent 10 years preparing for that moment and missed it by a split second.

The good news is you are probably not an Olympic athlete and that's good news because there is room at the top for everyone who reads this. But you have to know the rules.

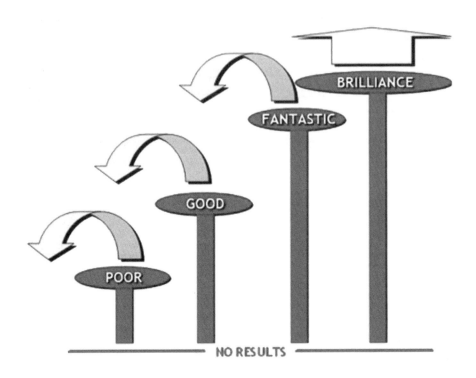

Take a look at a scale showing the results people get versus the effort they put in. As you can see at the base line you have a place called 'no results', nothing at all is happening.

Just above that base line you have a POOR job. Of course, if you do a poor job, the results you would expect to get would be poor. We don't want to do a poor job so let's go to the next level.

The next level after poor is doing a GOOD job. As I said before, who wants to do a good job? Not me, because as you can see from the model, when you do a good job these days, what type of results are you going to get? No not good! If only you were so lucky! You do a good job and you actually get POOR results. How do I know that? Because if you do a poor job you get NO RESULTS – you are out of business.

Can you imagine if you were running a hotel, managing a restaurant or co-ordinating a mail order company and you were consistently doing a poor job, how long would you last? Not very long at all. So, if doing a poor job means you are out of business, it makes sense that by doing a good job you will get poor results. This can be a little disheartening but the examples are everywhere.

What is the next stage? The next stage is to go even higher than good (we were talking about this word earlier) by doing a FANTASTIC job. When we do a fantastic job we would hope to get fantastic results but look at the model. We do a fantastic job and we only get good results. Ah ha! Has the penny dropped?

Many people and organisations spend their time working somewhere between doing a poor and a good job. Every so often they peak towards fantastic. The results come back and they are good, so what happens? They become disheartened and drop right down to where they were before, doing a good or a poor job. This can be frustrating for many people. You work so hard, you do a fantastic job but you only get good results. Check your pay slip – are you getting paid too much?

So looking at the model, is there anywhere else you can go? There is – a tiny fraction – a tiny difference. If you were to visualise it, it is only a few millimetres between fantastic and the next level which is called BRILLIANCE! And that is the key. True success and happiness is about not just doing a good job, not even doing a fantastic job; it is about doing a BRILLIANT job!

## Brill bit

Brilliance is about pushing that little extra, just going one further step, going the extra mile, caring more, understanding more, researching more, delivering more, and by applying that you will do a brilliant job.

Here is the most exciting part of the whole process. When you do a brilliant job you don't get fantastic results, you get brilliant results! The rewards are brilliant, the effect on others is brilliant, and your quality of life is brilliant.

If you understand the power of this concept, you'll also understand it's not where you want to be, it's where you must be.

You will want to do a brilliant job and receive brilliant results. However, the energy you have to put in to being brilliant is huge so this area must be vitally important to you or you will not give the commitment, energy, passion and enthusiasm that will be needed in order to achieve BRILLIANCE.

> **Brill bit**
>
> When you set a brilliant standard you have got to step up continuously. When you set a new standard for yourself and you understand why you want to be brilliant it keeps you on the edge at all times. That's where the fun and enthusiasm for life comes from.

What's the message? It's simple. If being brilliant at something is important to you, make an honest judgement about where you are on the Brilliance Benchmarking scale right now. Then ask, are you currently doing; a poor job, a good job or are you doing a fantastic job? Whichever one of those levels you find yourself on, the message is simple. Step up!

What's your response? 'I'm going to do that. I'll start next week'. Too late! Remember, massive action equals massive results. So do it now! Make a commitment to the areas in your life where you want to be brilliant and start right now.

Reproduced with permission © Pearson Prentice Hall 2004, 2007

*"It's no longer good enough to be good."*

## *Michael Heppell*

# 9

# Interview with Jo O'Neill
## Center Parcs

# Interview with Jo O'Neill,
# UK Training Manager, Center Parcs

*Jo joined Center Parcs in 1991. Her role initially was Training Manager at their first UK site at Sherwood Forest. During Jo's career in Center Parcs, spanning 16 years, the role has grown and developed as the company grew in the UK to 4 villages with 6000 employees.*

**MH** What are your expectations from a learning provider now and how would you see that changing in the next five years?

**JO'N** We are looking to re-profile our NES contract and so in order to expand we have got to look at how we are going to do that. We need a learning provider to be able to deliver the programmes we want, that's key to us. We want programmes that use our occupational standards. We don't want to be pushed into a direction of a framework that isn't right for us where people have got to do things that don't fit the job role. They very much have to fit our occupational standards.

**MH** Is there much of a compromise with that? Would you be happy saying 50% of a course is OK and fits directly but the other 50% is just part of the curriculum?

**JO'N** No, it has to be absolutely right for us. We made that stand with our Chef's Academy, dictating the way we want it to go. We wanted to offer more to the trade because we wanted to give them more than the job necessitates. We didn't want them to do things 'routinely' that are nothing to do with the job in hand. Our people have to do things in a fast process line and colleges cannot offer that. At college it's a nice steady pace and it is completely unrealistic to the job they've got to do.

**MH** And when they arrive with you it's very suddenly 'real life?'

**JO'N** Yes, exactly. We have been sending people to college for many years to do Food Prep. and Cooking qualifications and they would often say to their chef back at work, "What have I just done that for?" And the chef had to say, "Well you just have to do it". That's something we are not prepared to do any more. We are looking (from a provider's point of view) for a college/provider to deliver our occupational standards. We are looking for a consistent Contract's Manager who is flexible across a wide curriculum area. Center Parcs are very unique in that we have many trades here – every trade conceivable! We're not just catering. We're not just leisure. We're not just 'Technical Services' or water sports management; we have a whole wide range of trades. So if we are going to offer vocational awards at a basic level it would cross at least 6 or 7 disciplines. So that Contracts Manager has to work for us across the curriculum of our areas.

The other key thing, and this is a huge one, is flexibility. A provider needs to be flexible to our business needs; they need to come on the days and at the times it suits us. This is a big issue we have with colleges. We certainly need the assessors to come at the right times for us, to be very aware of our business needs and not be interfering with business. When we are under pressure they have got to be very much in the background and not interfering. They can observe but can't make themselves too obvious.

**MH** What is the value of your training contract?

**JO'N** At the moment it is £350,000 and we hope it will grow over the next three years to £750,000.

**MH** What are the three key things you look for when partnering with a college?

**JO'N** Business focused with an established work based learning team. We are partnering with four colleges. We made a decision at the beginning of our apprenticeship contract that we wanted to work with the colleges who were very much aligned to our Villages. We put our work out to tender. We interviewed and asked providers to demonstrate how they would manage the contract. We interviewed 6 or 7 colleges for 4 'positions' and every one was completely different, certainly in terms of what they wanted to charge us – utterly different. But the main thing is we wanted them to be business focused with an established work based learning team and that wasn't the case with every college we saw. We looked for good OFSTED inspections within the work based learning unit and a good leadership from a strong Contracts Manager within that college; someone we could be completely reliant upon to manage the contact for us, because we don't have the personnel in-house and we don't want to build an enormous in-house team.

We know what we want from our business. We know our people. We know what works and what doesn't. So we want to tell a college what we want, and we want them to be able to provide what we want. Then we need that relationship to build and grow with us and move beyond 'you tell us what you want'.

**MH** How do you know when a learner has been successful?

**JO'N** At the moment we are working with key learning providers as well as the four colleges and we have regular progress meetings with a spokesperson from the different colleges and their representative from the works learning unit. We will have agreed tracking documents with them and we obviously expect the tracking document to be maintained.

And for the learners directly, we would want to know that they felt they were getting value from what they were doing; that they were engaged in that relationship with the college. We would want to know that their manager felt that the assessors and the support from that college was sympathetic to the business need.

**MH** How do you gauge best value when it comes to buying training?

**JO'N** A lot of what we are doing is bench marked, so this is very interesting. When we interviewed the colleges we wondered how they'd come up with their pricing and how each compared for offering the same thing.

**MH** How different were they?

**JO'N** Radically different. In terms of how much they wanted to charge per day, it varied substantially.

**MH** Do the colleges appear to offer the same type of provision for that price?

**JO'N** Yes.

**MH** So would you go with the cheapest one?

**JO'N** Not necessarily.

**MH** Isn't that interesting. People think it's about price but I think it's about value.

**JO'N** It is all about value and it's about what we felt we would get in the relationship we were trying to develop. So West Suffolk is the most expensive and we negotiated hard, as we do at Center Parcs, and got them down to as low as they were prepared to go but they were considerably different to Kendal for instance.

**MH** So in terms of West Suffolk, what was it that made you feel it was worth paying that little bit more.

**JO'N** Probably because West Suffolk does stand out, and there really wasn't any other real contender in that region. As a Company we work very closely with West Suffolk, we have a lot of inter-linked relationships with them. Not just from the training perspective but also from an employment perspective; we entertain their students, they entertain our employees. They put forward students to us for positions, so we have got quite a good working relationship and that is something we at Center Parcs have always tried to foster with the colleges of our choice.

**MH** What mistakes does Further Education make that you wish they didn't?

**JO'N** My colleague has written here, 'the high hourly rates in tender submissions which are there to contribute towards the funding of FE'. What we are finding is the curriculum in some colleges still takes priority. So we see this sort of dichotomy. There seems to be curriculum – which is the main purpose, and work based learning – to support business. The colleges seem to distinguish those two areas quite separately. Where they have a focused Contracts Manager within work based learning, they become more business focused.

When it all becomes a bit watered down and curriculum takes priority, work based learning suffers, we suffer. We are obviously starting to compare what the college offers, compared to another training provider. I know that the NES don't want us to do that. They are very keen for us to foster our relations with a college. Could a single college offer us what a single provider could offer us? That's what we are considering for the furthering of our contract.

The main mistake I think colleges make is setting their rates too high, because we have a training provider who would under-cut a college and offer us a better service.

**MH** So when you find yourself in that situation, do you make a purely commercial decision at that point?

**JO'N** When we first went out to tender we had interest from seven colleges and also an external provider. The external provider's tender was a lot lower than the colleges, and we still went with the colleges. We felt that our decision was right for the Chef Apprenticeship Academy, which we wanted to get off the ground but our circumstances have changed. We are now going to 'concessions', part of our food and beverage operation is now going to a third party contractor, which has never happened in the history of Center Parcs. This downgrades the chef requirements we had a year ago. We need to consider whether to go with the provider who could offer us all that we need, or do we chase four colleges.

**MH** Would you have preferred the college's Contract Managers to have said, 'We know your requirements are changing, tell us what you are looking for and let us create something to fulfil that need, and stay with us'.

**JO'N** I don't think they are equipped in that way at the moment. I don't think they are that geared up. I don't believe they are that business focused.

**MH** If you were setting up a college right now, what three things would you focus on first?

**JO'N** Employer engagement and really understanding what it is we need and why. A strong business link, it's got to be a two-way process, having this strong link with us as a company and a main employer for the region. Simplified communication with tendering and paperwork; the paperwork side drives us round the bend as we are a very busy operation. Communication is very important to us.

**MH** You would obviously have to find teaching staff and support staff to work in this college. In the next five to ten years time, what would those people look like?

**JO'N** We believe that the best support we have had from the colleges so far is where staff come from industry. They have a working life experience not just 'cook class'. West Suffolk staff are very business focused and have come from industry. They appreciate the pressures we experience every single day, staff need to understand business.

**MH** Values versus skills; skills can be learned but values are something within you.

**JO'N** I know from my perspective we are involved in a lot of detail but people use so much jargon that at times I don't have the faintest idea what they are talking about. I don't want to keep saying every five minutes – well what was that then? There is so much jargon; not only the qualification, the framework, the funding, how they manage things. Center Parcs is bad enough for jargon! I think Center Parcs embarked on the NVQ route, (I've been here 16 years), probably 15 years ago when NVQ's were quite new. It was a complete nightmare; one person watching, one person observing; and another observing another, and it never achieved anything for us. We shut the door on it after that and I purposely shut the door on anything to do with vocational awards. The NVQ had such a bad name in Center Parcs we made a decision not to do anything at all and we have become very insular. I think we are very good at what we do and what we deliver and it has only been more recently that each Village has been allowed to do their own thing on a low level: small scale basis and that was generally with local providers. The reason we are interested now and we have gone for the national contract is the whole ethos has changed, which allows us to say what we want.

*"The future belongs to those who prepare for it today."*

**Malcolm X**

# 10

# The power of words

# The power of Words

Words define who we are. Spend five minutes with a couple of friends doing this simple fun exercise.

## Step 1 – Study the words below

| | | | |
|---|---|---|---|
| Accessible | Brilliant | Comfortable | Decisive |
| Energetic | Fun | Keen | Likeable |
| Moaning | Neurotic | Obsessive | Personal |
| Quick | Robust | Specific | Tactile |
| User-friendly | Vulnerable | Worldly wise | eXperimental |
| Youthful | Zippy | | |

## Step 2 – Take five words from the list which most accurately describe you

1) _____

2) _____

3) _____

4) _____

5) _____

**Step 3 – Now take the five which definitely don't describe you**

1) _____

2) _____

3) _____

4) _____

5) _____


**Step 4 – Now take the five which describe a brilliant futurist**

1) _____

2) _____

3) _____

4) _____

5) _____

**Step 5 – Discuss**


*"My future starts when I wake up every morning... Every day I find something creative to do with my life."*

### *Miles Davis*

# 11

# Interview with Jackie Fisher

## Newcastle College

## Interview with Jackie Fisher, Principal and Chief Executive, Newcastle College

*Jackie is a Board member of the Higher Education Funding Council for England and also chairs their Strategic Committee for Widening Participation. Jackie is also a Board member of One North East, the North East Regional Development Agency, and chairs their Education, Skills and Employability Committee, she is also a Director of Newcastle Gateshead Initiative, the Chair of DOTT07 and is a Regional Council Member of CBI.*

**MH** What are you doing right now to Future Proof your College?

**JF** What does 'future proof' mean in our turbulent environment?

**MH** Preparing now for what things might be like in 5 – 10 years time.

**JF** I'm appointing good people who are capable of looking ahead and planning.

**MH** How do you find those people?

**JF** A huge range of ways; interviewing, headhunting, talking to people who know good people; informal relationships which then turn into something more formal.

**MH** Is this for your Management Team or is this for all of the staff?

**JF** Certainly for the Management Team and I guess that other people are doing the same to recruit the best people they can to the College.

**MH** Who do you think your most important customers are going to be in 5 years time?

**JF** Exactly the same people who are coming to the College now, but maybe funded by different routes.

**MH** What would they look like in 5 years time? What would their expectations be, what would they be looking for from your organisation?

**JF** I think they would be looking for a cost-effective, high quality provision in a great environment with great teachers.

**MH** You've obviously made some huge changes in the last few years – the infrastructure of the College is extraordinary now – what else are you going to be working on in terms of the environment where learning will take place?

**JF** We are part way through a renewal and re-building, and building of new property and over the next 5/6 years we intend to complete the total rebuild of Newcastle College and our College in Skelmersdale.

**MH** What's the cost of all of that?

**JF** The total cost by the time we've finished will be close to £300 million.

**MH** Is that the biggest build in the UK?

**JF** There's no way I could check what other people have done in terms of their build. I don't know.

**MH** How are you going to continue to fund your future plans?

**JF** Through operating cost effective provision, investing the College's surplus in a building programme and seeking support from other partners.

**MH** Who do you see as your future partners?

**JF** I think our future partners are the Learning & Skills Council, Local Authorities, RDAs, DCSF, DIUS individuals and employers and key college partners.

**MH** What mistakes do you want to avoid making?

**JF** I don't look at the world like that. I think what you try and do is make the best decisions you can make which move the College forward positively, at the time when you have to make that decision. Looking back on those decisions, you may have chosen (with the new knowledge) to have done something differently but planning to avoid mistakes is not really something that I can actually understand.

**MH** You would rather have the vision and make the mistakes than avoid making the mistakes and not achieve the vision?

**JF** No – I'd rather think about what I think is the best thing to do for Newcastle College at any particular moment in time and to make the best decisions I can with the best information I can, supported by the best people I can recruit and to move forward on that basis. If, looking back on that process in 5 or 10 years time, you think to yourself that I should have done x or I should have done y, then that is a bit of an unreal process because if you were to have had the new information then you would have made different decisions anyway. I don't plan and manage in order to avoid mistakes. I plan and manage to do the best it's possible to do for Newcastle College.

**MH** What do you think the ideal future teaching staff and support staff are going to look like?

**JF** I think they're going to be highly committed and passionate about education and about the organisation they work in. I think they've got to be highly skilled and flexible. They are going to be very customer focussed and they're going to be philosophical and resilient in relation to the environment in which we work and the amount of change they have to manage.

**MH** What do you think the role of the future Principal is going to be?

**JF** To lead increasingly complex and diverse organisations.

**MH** What sort of challenge do you think you're going to face in the next 5 years?

**JF** That I'm going to face or the College is going to face?

**MH** You, as the Principal.

**JF** To maintain resilience in an increasingly complex environment. To remain alert and responsive to changes in that environment and to keep absolutely focussed on what is mission critical to the College and to deliver great learning to students.

**MH** If you were to start a new college now – a brand new greenfield site – what would be the first three things that you would focus on?

**JF** No idea. It's not possible is it? If you have no history, no market, no buildings, no staff, you haven't got a college. The basics of a college are students, recruiting students, having great staff, having great facilities.

**MH** So would they be the things you'd focus on? Having great staff, having great facilities and recruiting students?

**JF** No, no – I don't think it's a good question. It's not a question that I can engage with.

**MH** Is there any question that you wish I'd asked you this morning?

**JF** No

*"I don't plan and manage in order to avoid mistakes. I plan and manage to do the best it's possible to do for Newcastle College."*

**Jackie Fisher**

# 12

## Talent times

## Talent times

Further Education will become a fertile battleground for talent. The very best will soar, with opportunity being thrust towards them on a daily basis. The average will suffer. It will no longer be good enough to be good.

Managers will be the main opponents in this war, looking to attract the very best talent with a global market to choose from. As geography becomes less and less important, the opportunity to find the very best will become the preoccupation of most managers; only surpassed by the energy spent in retaining the best.

In five years time, if you haven't been headhunted it means you're not that good. Ouch!

*"In the future everyone will be famous for fifteen minutes." I'm bored with that line. I never use it anymore. My new line is, "In fifteen minutes everybody will be famous."*

**Andy Warhol, 1979**

# 13

# Interview with Gary Groom

## Redcar & Cleveland College

# Interview with Gary Groom, Principal, Redcar & Cleveland College

*Gary has been in Further Education since starting out as a lecturer in Doncaster in 1988. Gary has a clear philosophy, which has at its core the drive to create not just a place to learn and work but an organisation that engages people both emotionally and socially through life-changing experiences.*

**MH** What are you doing right now to Future Proof your College?

**GG** We are developing a brand new single campus development. We're putting in a lot of new technology; we're taking a much more mobile approach to learning using mobile technologies and flexible learning environments.

We're also going to have devices on loan so students will be able to use the technology both inside and outside the classroom.

We took a lot of notice of the JISC (Joint Information Strategy Committee) document, which was produced to show how learners learn best in terms of learning environments. It's about the sociology of learning as much as anything else – there's so much peer group support that goes on between students in more casual learning settings that needs tapping into. Outside, we've landscaped quite a big garden area at the back of the College which is going to have access to wireless networks so on fine day students can sit outside and work.

It's as much about relaxed styles of learning as it is formal. The transmission of knowledge and information between staff and students is magnified massively if the students are in the right environment. If one student hasn't understood the transmission, they can access that understanding from another student using different words and different approaches.

So we want to monopolise that and we're going to encourage learners to continue their learning outside of the formal structure as much as possible.

We're also doing an awful lot of work looking at the change culture. I'm undertaking a cultural change project with change agents inside the College to try and develop a much more customer relationship-based approach to the people inside the College – people being staff and students. I think one of the things we often don't do well is to manage our customer relationships as effectively as we might.

The learner experience has to be one that really exceeds expectations and it is one where the learners are really looked after as individuals. So it's much more about the individual and the relationship we have with that individual. And that goes for staff working together as well – treating each other much more as individuals.

**MH** Who do you think your most important customer is going to be in five years time?

**GG** The most important customer is going to be the same as it is today. That's every single person that we have contact with, the very second we make our first contact.

**MH** That's interesting because that's not necessarily the people who are signed up on your courses – it's every single person who you have a contact with.

**GG** The very second we first make contact and I said contact because it's not necessarily meeting them. I could have a phone call, receive an email, meet them, whatever. That person could be a current student, an employer who's thinking about putting people through to us, someone in the street when we're out there on a Saturday in the market place with the College promotional stand. The minute we connect with someone for the very first time we've got just one second, and that first contact can mean that they will or will not think about us for more than five minutes and to the point where they will engage with the College.

**MH** One chance to make a first impression!

**GG** Yes that's it. It doesn't matter how much strategy, how much segmenting of the market, economic regeneration, or analysis you do –the first time you meet someone, if that very first impression is wrong, you've blown it.

Also, on top of that everybody wants self-serve. In conducting a number of surveys over the years I have found that young people source information about purchase decisions (and about whether or not they want to come to a College) in certain priority orders. The preferred order seems to be: Internet, telephone call, publicly available literature, last of all meet somebody and speak to them. Young people seem less interested in coming in and speaking to someone in situations where they have instigated an enquiry for themselves. Whether they're shy, lacking in confidence or embarrassed – I don't know what it is, but they would rather sit at a computer or pick up a phone and request that information is sent to them but it seems they would rather not have to meet somebody face to face in the first instance.

**MH** How are you going to fund what you want to do?

**GG** First of all, continued successful delivery. If we're going to continue to generate income from an array of sources, be it private, direct, LSC, University, Government office or wherever – whether they're existing or newly developing forms of funding – or even if we don't know yet where the money is going to come from in the future, brand value and reputation is everything – because everyone wants to work with a successful College and everybody wants the best that's on offer.

Sometimes it's about value for money but it's *always* about quality and brand value. And I believe that very firmly.

**MH** What mistakes do you want to avoid making in the future?

**GG** We never want to score an own goal! You can really set yourself up; brand value and perception is hard to build and it just takes one person to score an own goal or to not quite deliver and meet expectations. That has a huge impact on the business.

It's a really hard question to answer. The worst mistake you can make is the one you know you could have avoided (with hindsight) – it's the one where you just think 'we didn't need to do that'. And I don't know what they all are yet and probably never will – I wish I did!

**MH** What are your ideal future teaching and support staff going to look like?

**GG** You mean other than extremely attractive!! I want people who absolutely love what they do, that have passion, that have commitment, that have energy, that have vision, that have ambition for their students and for themselves. I actually want people that have some drive – they are innately driven.

I like Tom Peters' view on this – you should go out there and look for strange people, quirky people, people who have got something different about them.

Ultimately, you want people that buy into the corporate ideology, which you hope no one should have a problem buying into because it's something that everybody can value because it just philosophically looks right.

One of the things we say is that we'd like our College to be a really exciting and dynamic place to learn and work – and I don't think anybody would object to that.

I think one of the things you know is going to happen is you're going to get knocked and battered a bit on the way and what you need in the team is resilience and you need people who say – right, I've been knocked down, I'm getting up again. Not – I'm hurt, I'm injured, help me – while floundering around. We want people who are going to say that that's not going to stop us – nothing is going to stop us because we believe what we're doing is right.

My word at the moment is 'gumption'. I love that word. I'm looking for gumption and spirit and energy and commitment.

**MH** Who do you think your future partners are going to be?

**GG** I think we're working more and more closely with schools, employers and other providers but things are changing and changing faster and faster. It feels like we're fast approaching synchronicity, that moment where everything seems to happen almost all at once.

From a business point of view, Government agencies or departments come and go and we'll move to develop partnerships and relations with them as they evolve. More and more and more though, and I suppose this is quite topical, FE colleges and private providers are forming key alliances. There is a growing need to form stronger networks between providers. So rather than competing, we're finding it even more important to collaborate. That's because a lot of the central Government initiatives are based around much bigger projects and some of the things we are bidding for are national or regional projects now and you just can't do it on your own.

So our partners in that sense are going to be other providers and that will include schools. Because of the 14-19 agenda, we're going to have to work much more in partnership with schools – we do already – but curriculum planning is going to be much more about the school/college integration.

**MH** And what about yourself and the role of the future Principal?

**GG** I'm like a football manager – I could be out of a job tomorrow! College Principals come and go, don't they.

**MH** Why don't you future proof yourself, Gary?

**GG** One of the most important things I've learnt to do – and I've only been a Principal for two years is that you always have to know that your next decision could be your last. Although it sounds really negative, the responsibility is massive (you don't realise that until you're in the job) and ultimately you could make a bad critical decision, there's a lot of risk but you have to get on with it. Nobody likes to make a bad decision but the one thing that you must do in this role is you must make decisions. Everybody else can dither about but at the end of the day someone's got to say – that's what we're doing, that's where we're going. The most important thing you can do is to ensure that the channels of information are widely open and that you're getting all the right information from all the right places all of the time.

I think you also need to make sure you've got a much more rounded and inclusive decision-making process. You can make the decision, but you can be an army of one; if you don't take people with you things just don't work. So at the end of the day you still need to be sure that you've managed to take people with you – the powers of persuasion can be everything at times.

From a personal point of view, apart from keeping in mind the fact you're only as good as your last success, I think you could spend so long worrying about so many things that you lose the plot. You've got to target key actions and decisions, then put your energy into those things that you are committed to driving and not let the 'red herrings' get in the way. I don't want to be distracted by what I call 'the noise'. There's too much noise and at the moment in education there's masses of 'noise'. You've got to identify what the key messages are and what's just 'noise'. It takes a while sometimes and you can easily be distracted. I think one of the key things for any Principal is to stay focussed, keep on message and don't get distracted by 'the noise'. That to me is critical.

**MH** What would happen if you had to start a brand new college on a greenfield site? What three things would you focus on first?

**GG** I would look at where it needed to be because people underestimate how important location really is. For all the virtual learning and online learning you can do, a very important part of the learning culture is the social aspect and people need to be with people and communicate with people. There is still a lot of need for a physical meeting place.

I think I would focus very much on how the learning is going to be wrapped around the central sociological community. In our new design we've created a hub-and-spoke model and the things that are going to be common and the things that are going to drive groups of people together are in the middle.

It's a bit like going to a big city with no sense of a centre. Where's the centre in Leeds? Where's the river with all the little bars and places where people socialise? Where's the big square where people meet? Where's the heart of the city? There needs to be a sociological centre because a college is a community and if you haven't got that, it's not complete. It needs a heart; it needs a hub or centre.

I need to know more about what's driving people in schools at the moment. I believe really strongly that not everybody's ready at the same time – that's why we have Further Education, we're here for when people are ready.

When the Government says you should leave school with 11 GCSEs of which all should be A* to C – there's a benchmark – what if you don't? What if you don't see the value of it from 14-16? What if you're ready at 20 and then at 20 you come back and you do all 11 or something equivalent and you get them then, all because at 16 you just weren't ready. That would be my philosophy about what we do. People come back, come back, come back but they come back when they're ready. How many times have you heard the adult learner say 'I wish I'd done this at school', or 'I wish I had paid more attention at school', 'I wish I'd done this earlier'. The fact is, they just weren't ready then and that readiness is clearly formed from some kind of intrinsic motivation which needs to be developed and triggered and those triggers or stimuli are just not the same for everyone for a variety of reasons.

So if I was really trying to hit the core of economic regeneration, social restructuring, I would say, let's let go of this concept of, 'you're 16 therefore you should achieve 'this' now and 'you're 14 – you've got to take option choices now',

We need to find the intrinsic motivators that switch on the right learning pathway, delivered in the right way for each individual learner at the right time so that people can make their decision at the right time for themselves. Nobody should be set up to fail; everyone can be successful at something.

*"We need to find the intrinsic motivators that switch on the right learning pathway, delivered in the right way for each individual learner at the right time..."*

**Gary Groom**

# 14

# Interview
# with Stephen
# Heppell
## www.heppell.net

# Interview with Stephen Heppell, www.heppell.net

*Stephen Heppell pioneered collaborative virtual learning spaces. Past projects range from the Guinness Book of Record's largest internet project in the world last century, through a community of 20,000 head teachers to the worldwide Think. com. A string of very large scale projects showed and still show just how seductive online learning communities could be and he started these in the pre-web days of the 1980's.*

**MH** What do you think people can do to future proof themselves in education?

**SH** They need to do three things. Firstly, be aware of the certainty of uncertainty and the constancy of change – everything is going to change around you – and the analogy I give is when you're at the airport, step on to and walk along one of those moving pavements and you come across a family that are standing still. They think they're moving forward and you think they're holding you up. The important thing is to build a sense of the pace at which you are moving forward; it will need to be at least as fast as or faster than the cultural context. It's too easy to delude yourself that you're going forward and yet the economy and so on – the social context and technologies – are all racing past you. That's the first thing.

The second thing might be something as simple as reference building, self-esteem or breaking the cycle of third generation unemployment. You've got to have a vision for your learners that is ambitious and lasting. The reason for this is, as change happens there is something like 360 degrees of possibility that you might take. In terms of direction, what the vision gives you is narrowing it down to, say, 45 degrees of possibility. That means that your chances of being wrong or your chances of wasting your efforts are massively reduced. The vision doesn't define your choices but it guides them. And also, if everyone buys into that vision it's a great motivator, otherwise you're always fire-fighting the consequences of wrong decisions. This happens especially in colleges where people are just trying to keep up with the latest change. Whereas, if you have a clear sense of a shared vision, you embrace the change because it's taking you to where you all want to be going, and faster.

And the third thing is that it has to actually be good fun. People are in work at colleges as administrators, lecturers and leaders and that's for life! The students pass through and they have a good experience but for the staff, they're there forever and if they're not getting absolute delight out of all this, it goes nowhere. Don't forget to enjoy it, and that means the best possible model of learning you can think of for your learners should be the one that you're using to move yourselves forward.

**MH** What do you think the future teacher or future lecturer needs to look like?

**SH** Basically what's happened in the 21st century is that all the edges have got softer so the subject you thought was yours now turns out to be overlapping lots of others – and the length of the day starts earlier and it finishes later, people text you on Saturday. They're probably having a chat in Facebook about learning with other people elsewhere in the world, when before it just used to be a national curriculum. All the edges have got softer and that means that everyone is out of their box and that means you just need to be a little more agile. Agility is a key word.

I think the other thing they need is to still be passionate about learning. I think before, we were passionate about subjects – motor vehicle mechanics, iambic pentameter or whatever – now they've really got to be passionate about learning too. The starting point is that they're learning professionals and learning in the 21st century is really complex. Making great learning is challenging especially when there are so many variables – but hugely rewarding.

**MH** How well do you think we're doing in the UK compared to the rest of the world in terms of preparing for the future of education?

**SH** My honest answer is that the countries that appear to be front runners are the smallest ones because they're agile but also because they're happy with who they are. New Zealand is happy being New Zealand, Scotland is happy being Scotland. They're not trying to use education to do social engineering and the problem with the big countries is that you end up using education to try and sort out disaffection or unemployment or 'Britishness'. So countries that are small and are comfy with who they are are going really fast. On the other hand, we're doing way better than France or Germany or the USA. So the front runners are maybe Sweden, Catalan Spain, Scotland, Wales, New Zealand, Singapore, some Australian states – they're little places really but we're actually doing rather well for a big country I think.

**MH** With reference to IT, what type of things can you see happening in the next five to ten years?

**SH** I think, mostly in learning, that people have too often harnessed technology for productivity. They've tried to do what they used to do but a little faster or a little cheaper or maybe with a bigger group. The big change now is that people are realising that they can use technology to do things completely differently and it turns out they can be 300-400% more effective by doing things differently. Policy makers used to be happy with being slightly better year on year, like when pc's were introduced to help with writing skills. You get 20% better the first year, 10% better the second year and 5% after that, it's marginal.

On the other hand, when you're talking about children communicating or college students communicating, then the way that they're doing it with Facebook, video, YouTube, PSP's, phones, etc, it's just breathtaking. So the cool thing is to do it differently or look for entirely new ways to do it. A lot of what we did before was just about being slightly better and that doesn't really help at all.

**MH** People who have massively embraced technology have got amazing results, can you give me an example of someone?

**SH** There are so many. I was looking at a school in Australia where they had amazing results just one year after changing the way they taught: 87% improvement in teacher effectiveness, 80% gain in student morale, 61% improvement in student behaviour. This is not just to do with technology – you've got to have much bigger timetable blocks, you've got to have more open-ended learning, you've got to have more project-based work. There are a whole lot of things you can do. But, if you just embrace technology, you end up only with that stale and ineffective productivity model.

The ones who have made the best results have used technology as a Trojan horse to change everything and by changing everything they've got amazing results, really really impressive numbers. I've seen that in the schools in Australia, the Caribbean, Iceland, and Scandinavia... in a number of places.

There isn't a perfect answer out there, there is no recipe you can pick up and say "let's do exactly that in Nottingham" or wherever. There are lots of ingredients that people have tested worldwide and which have worked for them and I think we can use some of those ingredients and build local recipes but each recipe is going to be different because each college, each school is in a different culture and context.

**MH** What's exciting you right now?

**SH** The sheer speed of it all. Silly little example but I was on the train the other day going to Birmingham to a conference and 'Google alerts' pointed me to a blog by someone I'd spoken to in Scotland a week before. He'd posted about something I'd referred to where we broke a large school up into four smaller ones, with great success, in the Caribbean. I mentioned this to my travel companion whom I'm working with in the Caribbean. At that precise moment he was reading an online newspaper from the Caribbean that had just been published (this was 4am in Caribbean real time) and he was reading something about that very thing in the paper – an interview with the students. So I commented on the blog by pointing to that link. I get to the Birmingham conference – which was live-linked to Hong Kong – and I find out the chap introducing my keynote had also used 'Google alerts', so that he too had found that blog which he referred to in his introduction. Inevitably, I then showed it live in my talk. At this point my Caribbean pal, who I'd travelled up with and was sitting in the audience, takes a picture and posts it on his national "Building better futures" blog, which was due to be "launched" that very morning by the Education Minister, whose speech included the line that, "the world is watching" and shows the new blog which includes a picture of me at a conference in Birmingham, flagged by a Scottish blog, all referring to the newspaper that the Minister has not yet even had time to read and which came out just that morning.

Remember, the conference I'm at in Birmingham is paired with a conference in Hong Kong so suddenly the work he's about to announce has already been once round the world – the world is watching indeed! That's pretty cool, it's exciting stuff.

**MH** You have to be excited by it otherwise you'd be terrified by it!

**SH** It's a very bottoms up thing. We've got rid of the days when the people at the top told you what to do. Now people are discovering what to do by doing what you and I are doing now – using technology to swap ideas with each other. I think that's fab.

**MH** A lot of the work that you do is with schools, a lot of the work I do is with FE; FE says it's more difficult for us, it's easier for schools. Would you agree?

**SH** Yes and no. It is harder for FE because they've left it almost too late. The problem with the productivity thing is that you pin yourself into a corner because you're trying to get another 5% gain but you've had all the 5% gains that there were. There's no place left to go apart from desperation. And too many in FE have not left themselves enough space to "think differently". The institutions that can think differently have been able to pass right round the problem because most education is underperforming, often massively. But the lucky ones have still got just enough space left to be able to innovate. I'm involved in a lot of stuff in universities at the moment, pretty much building the equivalent of a whole campus at Bournemouth for example, and the problems are not so different from FE: productivity has eclipsed ingenuity and creativity.

**MH** What type of advice do you give whilst helping people design learning space?

**SH** There's a lot and it's complex. Agility is a key concept because you don't know what tomorrow is like – the certainty of uncertainty and so on. For example, there's a lot of stuff coming through about making Science teaching more effective through injecting performance – Dance and Drama – rather than just rarefied "pure" Science. It works. We wouldn't have anticipated that five years ago. If you build places around that are agile areas that don't have benches bolted down, you can have an area that's good for Science but by the way you can also do Drama there – so it's all about agility. And also try and take out the industrial scale stuff. Those hideous toilets that we build that process people's mass-weeing – and usually have a special ante-chamber apparently designed for bullying! And also PLEASE never build another corridor; we know in the future people will move around less, so why would you waste 20% of your college building resource developing special places to move them around when they're not going to be moving? If you get your eyes on the horizon you'll save a lot of money. But there are a million details – if it was simple, we'd have already got better buildings and currently they are scarce.

**MH** Are there any questions that you wish I'd asked you today?

**SH** The big one is 'Why would you bother with all this? Why not just carry on like it was before?' The simple answer is because this is what our generation should do. I think our Grandparents made a big difference with medicine. My honest belief is that we can do with learning what our forefathers did with medicine. This is our business, it's our generation – it's what we do.

You look at the rest of the world – it's not going so well at the moment is it? If we can get learners working together around the world and understanding each other rather than killing each other then that's hopeful. For example, I know we can "inoculate" children against poverty through learning – I've seen it work.

*"My honest belief is that we can do with learning what our forefathers did with medicine. This is our business, it's our generation – it's what we do."*

**Stephen Heppell**

# 15

# 12-year-old entrepreneurs

# 12-year-old entrepreneurs

My good friend Professor John MacBeath OBE, who is Chair of Educational Leadership at Cambridge University, told me an amazing story which I believe speaks volumes for the future of education.

On a recent visit to the United States, John was working in a school helping them with the implementation of some of their progressive education plans. At the end of his time in the school a 12-year-old boy introduced himself and handed John his business card; it read –

**Curtis L. Taylor, CEO**
**Dynatronics**

**For all your Internet, IT and Development Needs**

John was intrigued by this and asked the boy to describe his business. His claim to fame was that he had written a development plan for the school's IT future and presented it to the senior staff. They were now using it as a basis for upcoming development.

Astounded, John went to speak with the Principal of the school. Sure enough he confirmed that indeed this young entrepreneur had written the development plan and they were using it. In addition, he'd also offered to conduct a 2-day intensive training programme for all staff to show them how to apply the ideas and get the most from his the ideas.

"That's amazing", said John, "are you going to use him?"

"We would love to…" the Principal replied, "but we can't afford his fees!"

*"Whoso neglects learning in his youth, loses the past and is dead for the future."*

*Euripides (484 BC – 406 BC)*

# 16

# Interview with Rob Badcock

## with Rob Badcock

### Milton Keynes College

# Interview with Rob Badcock, Principal and Chief Executive, Milton Keynes College

*Rob Badcock has been the Principal and Chief Executive of Milton Keynes College since 2003. Prior to joining the College, Rob was the Chief Executive of Milton Keynes Manpower Forum, a work-based learning provider. Since graduating with a BA Hons in Scandinavian Studies at the University of Newcastle-upon-Tyne and working as a translator in Sweden. Rob has enjoyed a career in the learning and skills sector spanning some 30 years.*

**MH** What are you doing right now to Future Proof your College?

**RB** I think that the starting point is that you are here to be successful in what you do. And that really boils right down to the work that you do with students. No matter how many partnerships you have, what the state of your buildings are, how your finances are doing, whether or not you have a view on the new machinery of Government – if you are running a successful FE College then people will want to do business with you at all levels.

**MH** How are you defining success?

**RB** Obviously we have to take the student success measures against which we are judged – retention and achievement. But it goes broader and deeper than this. The perception of the College is critical – the way students, parents, employers, partners and key stakeholders view you. Add all those up and you've got a weight of opinion, haven't you? You have a body of credibility – people who will be not only your advocates and allies but champions if the going gets tough. At an important partnership board meeting not so long ago, an employer criticised the College for not meeting the needs of business. I was about to open my mouth to respond but was beaten to the mark by three other people defending us to the hilt. That's the best! That doesn't happen unless you are actually successful and people can touch and feel what you do with your students. For me that is where it starts and finishes.

We're also talking about reputation management here. When Foster was beginning to share his findings, we took a strategic decision to invest further in how we profile ourselves. I appointed a marketing professional as Vice Principal; he in turn brought in a marketing manager from outside the sector. These two guys have taken us onto a different plane over the past two years.

We were fortunate enough to win an FE First Marketing Award and also two Heist Awards, which recognise excellence in FE and HE. We could only do that because we felt really confident about what we were saying and doing. It cannot be a question of design over function.

**MH** Somebody once said to me 'Best Product but Shut' is not what you want on your epitaph.

**RB** Absolutely. You need to know where the market is going. Future proofing is about understanding the direction of the market and how you will respond, whether it's adult learning, offender learning, Higher Education. You have to be able to read the runes. And it goes back to what I said before, if we have mixed press, we'll be seriously put to the test in a competitive climate.

I guess the other side of that is if you are good, then you have to make sure that people know about it. As a sector we excel at hiding our light under a bushel.

**MH** How do you go about doing that?

I think it's really interesting, because you make assumptions. And sometimes they are false assumptions. You assume that those who are closest to you know you. But actually, when you test your close partners and stakeholders, they sometimes don't really know what you do at all!

And given that your best customers are repeat customers and will themselves act as advocates, it really is quite important that they understand what you do, isn't it?

As Principal I target key people in the private, public and voluntary sectors and hold myself personally responsible for managing their 'account'. The best thing we have invested in however is the use of students as ambassadors. Our successful campaign last year was based on a 'Big Idea': "The voices and faces of our students will be the voice and face of Milton Keynes College". The whole campaign was built around students telling the story and that contributed to a 23% increase in 16-18 year olds walking through the door.

**MH** Who are your most important customers going to be in five years?

**RB** We will continue to be major players in the youth market, which will get younger. The advent of the diplomas and department changes will mean a new relationship basis with schools and local authorities. We as a college will certainly be expanding Higher Education and of course have plans to set up a University Centre, work with employers will continue to be centre stage.

**MH** How are you going to fund the future plans that you have, I guess you've got some big plans, how will you fund them?

**RB** Yes we do have some big plans. Partly because we are ambitious for our students and partly because the city itself has big growth plans. I don't know how much you know about Milton Keynes, but we are already the largest city outside London in the South East and are expanding at a rate of 2,500 new homes a year. That takes the city to the size of Bristol in about twenty year's time.

So an important part of my job is to ensure that LSC planning takes this growth into account when allocating student numbers. The city also acknowledges that the College is a key component of the infrastructure and assists us with capital investment.

The boundaries between FE and HE are shifting and I see the development of Higher Education as an exciting prospect. Clearly the ability to validate our own Foundation Degrees will be an important step on the road towards HEFCE funding.

**MH** Moving forward now what mistakes do you want to avoid making on that journey in the next five to ten years?

**RB** I'm not sure whether this neatly fits your question, Michael, but I want to say something about partnerships. The word partnership is written large on every piece of guidance, legislation etc that comes down from on high. I've been around for long enough to know that if a partnership is 'commissioned', then there may be trouble ahead. Partnerships really have to be on your own terms. Don't get me wrong, we have some cracking partnerships in place, which really add value. Then there are some, which you feel ambivalent about, and then the odd couple, which may take a lot of time and energy to unravel.

Partnership is the easiest thing to say and one of the hardest to do.

**MH** And the second mistake to avoid?

**RB** The older I get the clearer I am on this. If deep down inside you know that something isn't working – for your students, for your college – you have to act swiftly and decisively. It could be a partnership issue; it could be a staffing issue. Life's too short.

**MH** Let's have a look at staff. What do the ideal future staff look like for you in terms of teaching staff and support staff?

**RB** If you are clear on the direction you wish the College to take, there needs to be a cultural fit. I recently heard a fellow Principal, Ioan Morgan talk at a conference about the 'Warwickshire Way' and I know exactly what he meant.

Can I come from another angle?

Like all colleges, we run all sorts of reports on our staff body. I think it was about twelve months ago that we pressed a different button one day and it told us that over 11% of our staff in MK are ex-students. That surprised us, only because we hadn't asked the question before.

We have over 12,000 local students a year and I am sure we don't push opportunities in the College enough. We know our core reason for being is to enable students to progress – we just assume it's to somewhere else.

**MH** So will you set up something so people go through that process and you give them an option to work with you at the end of it?

**RB** I would like to think so. It's part of a larger piece of work to really understand why and how our staff choose to come to us.

One of my students at this year's Awards Ceremony told me he'd like to stay at College and work as a Student Ambassador. He said he would like to 'give something back'. I had to smile at his choice of words. I associate 'giving something back' to retired footballers or boxers, not a 19 year old. But it was nice nonetheless…

Succession and planning has to be at the heart of future-proofing. We've been hearing about the dearth of potential Principals for a number of years now. I have a senior team of one Deputy Principal and three Vice Principals. They all have the talent to become Principals themselves. I also see strong potential at director and middle management level coming through in the College. We have engaged actively in peer referencing projects over the past five years, which involves our staff visiting other colleges on a regular basis. And of course, there is the risk then that staff have a good close look at other colleges and are attracted by them. My view is that if I have to lose them, I'd rather lose them to the sector.

**MH** Looking at partners is a big area for FE. Who do you think your future partners are going to be?

**RB** Well I think the balance of partnerships will change and that will be a challenge. The Local Authority assuming responsibility for under-18 provision and the roll-out of diplomas will bring a strong focus to the locality, which is a good thing. We will clearly have to manage the relationships with schools with the same level of investment that we are committing to other partners at the moment.

**MH** Do schools see you as a threat?

**RB** Yes, I guess they do. A new school is being built each year in MK and all the schools have sixth forms, so it can be competitive.

Having said that, the 14-16 initiatives have been excellent in bringing us closer. When you have fellow professionals from both sectors engaging in positive discussion around an individual student, then you know you're on the right road. To my mind, Increased Flexibility has arguably been the most effective intervention of recent years. And yet it's been the under-funded, unsung hero. Genuinely life-changing, and at the right age, many of the youngsters would have been lost to the system. Our conversion rate has consistently been above 60% and I know this is not uncommon in the sector.

The other area where I believe partnerships will strengthen is with Universities. At a local level, we are currently putting the final touches to plans to establish a University Centre for Milton Keynes and that's an exciting prospect for our students.

It goes without saying that our work with employers will continue to hold centre stage and I think it's important to play a lead role on this front. I have a personal target to establish six key accounts each year and I do that at MD level.

**MH** How do you set up business partnerships?

**RB** It's a question of knowing how people do business. You create a relationship based on how you can help each other and people are genuinely open to it. Once you get them into the College they almost always say 'this is amazing, I never knew you did this'.

Foster spoke of the need for specialisation. I'm not so sure. Let me give you a case in point.

I invited the Manager of a major city centre hotel into our training restaurant for lunch. He was looking for staff. We started off exploring how we could help him in the kitchens and in the restaurant. We then moved on to front-of-house staff. He asked, almost as an aside, 'where would I go to get a trainee accountant?' I said 'you don't go anywhere, you come to us'. 'And where would I go to get a youngster for our maintenance team?' 'You don't go anywhere, you come to us'. And the conversation went on. It wouldn't have been as 'employer responsive' if I were not able to offer the broad range of service.

I find myself increasingly spending more of my time with students on the one hand, and with leaders of organisations on the other. The balance is not easy to strike, but it feels just about right at the moment.

**MH** Your role as Principal in the future, is that really to build those relationships?

**RB** Absolutely. If Foster did one thing it was to put reputation management near the top of every Principal's list. The other part of my job title is Chief Executive, and that's about running a sound business that clearly knows where it's going and is not subject to peaks and troughs.

**MH** So forget that you have Milton Keynes College and imagine there is a brand new college that you are going to open. What three things are you going to focus on first?

**RB** I know what the number one is without thinking. Maybe I'm less sure of the other two.

The number one focus has to be staff. I would want to build an excellent body of staff around me. I'm really fortunate with the team at MK College, at all levels. If I had to focus on one layer, it would be middle-management. There is such a strong correlation between good student success and a good head of department and the reverse of that coin is certainly true. That's where positive leadership really has an impact.

The second is more wish-list than focus, and that would be location; probably because my three campuses are rather tucked away from public view.

And the third, not too sure. Give me a fine body of staff in a shiny new building at the top of the hill and I'll start from there…

*"Change is the process by which the future invades our lives."*

**Alvin Toffler**

# 17

# Rocks to the Surface

# Rocks to the surface

I was out for a run with my wife in the beautiful Northumberland countryside. After an hour we stopped for a rest and watched as a farmer scoured his field looking for and removing rocks. Some were huge! I asked him how long it would take to clear the field and he smiled as he responded with, 'a few days!'

'I bet it's worth it to end up with a nice clear field', I offered.

'Well it is, but I'll have it all to do again next year!' He went on to explain that rocks find their way to the surface through time and if he didn't take time out to clear the field he'd have a heck of a bill for the damage they'd do to his farm machinery at harvest time.

I suppose we all have our rocks which come to the surface; usually in the form of people who would be happy to cause damage and problems right when we should be reaping the rewards of a good harvest.

Who are those people in your life or organisation?

Just as the farmer needs to have a clear out every year, I would suggest you do the same. I noticed that the farmer didn't throw all the rocks away. He kept some, for fixing walls, some he just tipped at the side of the field out of harms way.

It's an unwritten law that even if you do manage to get rid of the rocks, just as the farmer does, you will have to do it all again 12 months later. The key is the timing. The farmer removed the rocks before he planted the seeds. He 'future proofs' his fields for harvest. It's hard work at the time but he's working towards something better.

I dare you to clear your rocks – now.

*"A cynic is not merely one who reads bitter lessons from the past, he is one who is prematurely disappointed in the future."*

**Sidney J. Harris**

# 18

# Interview with Peter Gilroy

## Kent County Council

## Interview with Peter Gilroy OBE, Chief Executive, Kent County Council

*Peter has worked in the public and private sector in the UK and USA and has a national reputation for innovation. He is a member of the World Health Care Congress Advisory Board and chairs the Kent Film and Television Board.*

**MH** What are your expectations from a learning provider now and how can you see that changing in the next 5 years.

**PG** One of the problems at the moment is that the performance of FE colleges is prescribed by central Government and this leads to tensions when you are trying to reignite the South East economy. You want the colleges to be centre stage in the process but that doesn't fit with a tick box mentality in Government, which also has an effect on their money streams. So if, for example, I want to get a college to take an aggressive stance on creating high quality training for the marine industry around one of the ports, but that does not fit the Government's agenda then although they might well put something in their curriculum, it tends to appear as an afterthought because their main funding has to be committed elsewhere.

How are we doing now? If I am honest, I don't think that the system is fit for purpose for the 21st Century at the moment, and this is no disrespect to the colleges. I think the process of transformation that is taking place in the economy, certainly in this region, requires a much more dynamic process and totally freeing up. This is not about their principles or their competence; this is about the way in which their business is constrained by what is essentially a highly centralised dictat and I think that is ultimately doomed to failure.

Now the future, well I expect to see a radical shift – whether that is to do with economic hubs; or a totally new approach to access, or a much more creative relationship with the private sector and industry, and I don't just mean good relationships but I mean sharing each others assets more dynamically – having people from business in colleges, and vice versa; developing exchange programmes more dynamically. As a provider, when you are talking about how you deal with an individual going through the system, it needs to be much more personalised, much more outcome-focused and much more geared to the changes that are taking place in the local industrial base in the economy.

There has got to be seamlessness in the future. A new cultural face in my view in relation to colleges both for FE and Higher Education. That means brand new relationships, it means a whole new way of thinking about training and that's pretty transformational if we can do it. It may mean clustering different skills around particular colleges to focus energy and attention on outcomes. The FE colleges and local Government should see themselves as facilitators, focusing talent on local economic demand.

**MH** When you partner up with a college, what type of things are you looking for?

**PG** A good example would be a partnership we have at the moment with the film industry in Kent. We have increased our investment in that industry. Now we need to get the young people who may not have gone through Higher Education into that industry. How do we do that? The creative industries can tend to be rather a mercurial industrial base and so you have got to have a very dynamic interplay. As an example, we have just become an Executive Producer for a film which will go on general release in due course. We did this to make sure that a local film company could stay working and filming in Kent. Now we are the first Local Authority to do this. As part of the deal I wanted them to take a group of young people from the local college full time into the production aspects of the film, as runners or whatever and to start moving on a dynamic NVQ base, getting that connection with the colleges right on day one. That is really difficult, but I would want to go a step further than that, I would be saying that we should have a consortia relationship with a cluster of colleges and even the lecturers would start to change. In other words we would have people from the industry who would be part of the college and part of the industry. So it would be a totally different type of structure and a much looser, outward-looking structure rather than an inward-looking one.

It requires new competencies and new ways of working both for the industry and the colleges and a very different and much closer relationship. So when you start talking about the personalisation of services in learning, it is not simply about harnessing the ICT issues – which is very significant in Kent at the moment – and trying to get collective learning through interactive technology, which is obviously another big dimension for the future; but changing the way in which we work out new partnerships and work out new agreements, so that, for me, is part of the future. The relationships need to be very creative and this will be of particular significance for SME's

Another example is to do with Principal leadership and management training. I have started a leadership programme here in Kent where all of the public sector – fire, police, health, local government – and major players in the private sector have come together to become part of the programme. It is run in conjunction with the Tanaka Business School, the University of Kent Business School and the Business School of Virginia in America. We had never done this before. When I went into colleges they said 'what's this about' and I explained it's actually a new way of doing business. We are going to have senior people from the private sector and the public sector going through an 18 month programme with action learning which is international. It is based on self-learning and it is a new way of doing business.

The journey was quite extraordinary. You would think in terms of relationships that it would be fairly easy. But actually it wasn't. But in the end they got very excited by the 'world is flat stuff'. That is a lateral view of the world and involves everyone moving away from their territory, their comfort zones, and being much more outcome federated and focused. We are all going to move away from our silos.

We have gone through three tranches so far and not only are they 'blue sky' but the learning is amazing. If you are in an academic setting, it is critically important in my view for the future that you have more time out; that your world is not set within the confines of the college. That sounds trite but frankly it means walking it in a very different way. So that is my view of the future.

**MH** Think about the learner, how do you measure success for a learner now and how do you think that might change again in the future.

**PG** The way I view it is in terms of outcomes. Does that person have the right competencies? Does that person have the ability to get into the employment market? I don't mean they have to be high flyers but; are they adequately, in qualitative terms, getting good advice. I am very critical of that at the moment. People giving the advice need to be very well informed and in tune with business. Then people need to have a sound social skills footing and the ability to form constructive relationships as a basic template for employment. This is of critical importance but I feel it is somewhat lost in the centralised performance framework.

Whether it is about new apprenticeships, or the quality of apprenticeships, in the various industries; local Government, the health service, all of us are taking that very seriously.

For me the test is what's the outcome? What's the competency? And in the end do they have a fulfilling job? If people are going to be changing jobs over the next 25 – 30 years in the way we think they are, then we must make sure they start with a good base. We are now more purposeful; we're not talking about just the 17 pluses or the 19 pluses, or the 21 pluses we're talking about the 14-24 age group and getting a much more open system for youngsters to move in and out of the school base from 14 in a way that gives them experience which is much more relevant to their future.

**MH** What are you looking for in terms of best value if you buy training from an FE establishment?

**PG** I suppose there are 3 main things. One is, are they sufficiently incentivised and able to move, shake and change fast.

Secondly, have they got continuity of competencies and relationships in value terms in doing the work that you ask them to do. That means moving away, in my view, from a checklist mentality.

Thirdly, are they seriously working out how they personalise learning, and that includes what is in their business framework. In my view, the application of new technologies is fundamental.

**MH** What mistakes do you think FE makes now that you wish they didn't?

**PG** I think we've got into a cultural base nationally where a Government, unwittingly, has got into a belief, a sort of cultural norm of acceptance, that centralised prescription on FE is the way forward. And what that's done, paradoxically is seriously disempowered Principals and it's disempowered the notion of innovation and managing risk. I would expect any good FE college to be really high on innovation. In other words they should be able to take risks; they should be able to experiment with us as purchasers and learners on new ways of doing things. I think structures in Government have got to let go. The present way of thinking, and I accept this is a personal view, disempowers colleges. In the end it does not work, it kills off creativity; it kills off motivation and it is a mistake. Difference should be seen as a strength, not a weakness.

**MH** If you had a job of setting up a college now, what 3 three things would you focus on first?

**PG** Firstly I would focus on the key emerging economies, both nationally and locally.

Secondly I would focus, before getting into structures and form, on what relationships I would be demanding of my staff in relation to the economy. I include all the public services in that, not simply the private and NGO world.

The third issue is in terms of its design. It may actually be a virtual college and not a traditional college build because I would be expecting all of my staff to have a much more common sense approach to the way in which people gain competencies generically in the system. If we're going to go for an NVQ type process, let's go for that and make it sensible, make it real. If we're going to give them other opportunities, then there needs to be a serious connection with what that experience has actually meant for them – it is not simply about credits, it is actually the relevance of what they have been doing and how that fits into any new curriculum or new pathway in the academic world.

**MH** What would your ideal future teaching staff look like?

**PG** There needs to be a different reward system in the whole of the economy. I would love to see a few of them better paid, fewer people but better paid with incentives, with a reward package; based on productivity, based on quality but looking after them and giving them a sense of value and having a highly decentralised structure that individual lecturers, individual people in the business are liberated and have much more freedom.

In our business we have a highly devolved system and the front end can make very important strategic decisions without referring back to the bureaucracy of the system, and I would like to see a bit more of that.

I would also like to see more fresh blood. A year ago I re-structured a Policy unit in Kent County Council which had 20 people. It now has 4 core people in there and we have an outer ring of people. I have people from the private sector, I have people from the voluntary sector and it's like an amoeba – it is always alive and always dynamic because the body is always moving but the core group stay. The unit is fluid and fit for purpose with change as a norm. So it is a model of having a core group of highly competent well paid people who are there to do the business

– Relationship Managers, Customer Managers and specific people who are there to motivate and create learning in different environments. Then you look after them well, and if you look after this smaller group of well-paid staff, it becomes a major opportunity.

*"The future is here. It's just not widely distributed yet."*

**William Gibson**

# 19

# Eight ways to prepare for and relish future competition

# Eight ways to prepare for and relish future competition

It wasn't until I got a new toothbrush and compared it to the one I'd been using for the last few weeks that I realised how worn out my old toothbrush had become.

Later that day I bought 2 new tyres for my car and it was only when I saw the old worn ones next to new ones that I realised how worn they were.

That night I attempted to find my electric screwdriver in the garage and ended up throwing out and giving away 4 bags of things I don't use any more. For the first time in years I had clear shelf space and the garage felt clean. It wasn't until I cleared the shelf that I realised how much junk I'd been storing.

We have never lived at a greater time for opportunity and prosperity. Look to the future; it's only going to get bigger and better.

However, with this comes greater competition than we have ever experienced. With a shrinking world, superior technology, faster pace and higher demands, competition will come in many forms.

The challenge is, most people find a way to adapt, or get by, and do not realise there is a better way (or a firmer toothbrush!)

So with so many opportunities, yet so much competition, what are the solutions?

**1)** Become multi-skilled. By learning multiple skills you will always be in the right place at the right time and ready to exploit every given situation. By developing a compulsion to learn you will fine tune your current skill set too.

**2)** Make Brilliance your Benchmark (see Chapter 8). If you have heard me speak or experienced one of our live events, you'll know this is one of my passions! Brilliance doesn't happen by accident. When you set a new standard it automatically becomes a must to erase the old and replace with new.

**3)** As Lord Baden-Powell said, Be Prepared! Outsmart the competition with your amazing insight and immaculate preparation!

**4)** Aspire to greatness. You become what you think about the most. What are you thinking about? Focus on your success. Feel it. Create an emotive link.

**5)** Take a risk (see Risk it for a Biscuit, Chapter 2). If you're hitting bulls-eye every time, you are probably standing too close to the target. Keep your 'risk' muscle in shape by trying new things.

**6)** Get rid of excuses. When the Spanish explorer Cortez landed at Vera Cruz, the first thing he ordered was for his crews to burn their ships. He then announced, 'you can fight or die'. This removed the third alternative of quitting. What can you do to remove your excuses?

**7)** Simplify what you are doing. While I was writing 'How to Brilliant' my editor said to me, 'Michael, I love most of Chapter 5 – other than the ending', 'What's wrong with the ending?' I asked. 'It should be closer to the beginning' she offered! What can you cut out?

**8)** Don't wait until your breath smells, your teeth are yellow and you've got spinach in the gaps. Get a new toothbrush! Get some new ideas, sign up for a course (do you know a good college?), listen to an audio learning CD, read a book, meet some funky new people.

Make it a must to prepare now for fierce competition because until you do, you won't even know what you don't know. And you're future competitors are going to love that!

*"The trouble with our times is that the future is not what it used to be."*

**Paul Valery**

# 20

# Interview with Mark Dawe

## Oaklands College

# Interview with Mark Dawe, Principal and Chief Executive, Oaklands College

*Mark became Principal of Oaklands College in August 2005. Previously Deputy Director in the DfES working in areas of FE policy and Skills for Life. Qualified as a Chartered Accountant with KPMG and worked for 7 years at Canterbury College as Head of Corporate Services.*

**MH** What are you doing to Future Proof your College?

**MD** I suppose the key things are; we have a new build coming through which allows us to design a facility which provides for future styles of delivery.

**MH** What particular styles of delivery?

**MD** The concept I've started with is there are no walls until someone justifies them, so this allows staff the opportunity to look at different designs and how they might want to deliver in the future rather than being constrained by classrooms or any other physical resource. We sent all the staff out to look at different designs; we have had capital champions in each area who have explored different things and different ways of delivering. That is very important in such a big building project.

Also we have no computer rooms in that facility so every learner gets a laptop. The whole IT side of things is different, we are doing a lot of work on that; for example, we've e-mentors which are students who are teaching the staff about the internet, what they can use from the web and how to use 'e' more in lessons.

**MH** So students are teaching the staff?

**MD** Yes, more as mentors.

**MH** How does the staff take that?

**MD** Initially there were some reservations, but actually it's a system we've used a lot now, and where the mentors have been used well we've seen dramatically improved results. There are certainly some good things happening.

**MH** When you say you are 'designing without walls' what are some of the ideas that people have come up with?

**MD** Different spaces and flexible spaces; maybe a row of three rooms without the back walls and then an open area behind so they can still have a relatively sound proof area for some basic teaching but can break out of the area behind. It's more of an overall resource area for one of the academic areas rather than just a row of classrooms and you're not quite sure what's in each one.

There are new contracts for staff with no contact hours, so again, looking at the future in terms of flexible delivery, more of a 'work load' approach. And on the business support side we are seriously looking at shared services and how we might be able to benefit this service we provide within the College through a shared services approach.

**MH** And have you got that set up now?

**MD** Shared services will literally debate with the LSC and others about them

**MH** How responsive is the LSC?

**MD** Very responsive because they want to see it happen

**MH** In five years time who will be your most important customer?

**MD** Well I suppose it's the student really, isn't it?

**MH** What type of student?

**MD** I think clearly 14-19 will be critical. I would see us being the vocational lead so the schools are our customers in terms of looking to us to provide the expertise wherever possible. Then in the adult market, obviously I would be foolish not to say the employer, but the employer and the individual I think are both equally important. The employer has his own business needs, the individual has career needs and the career need is not always what the employer is looking for. I think we will play a role in balancing the two; being able to help the employer develop their staff for their own business but then offer a broader qualification or whatever for the individual if they want to enhance what they are doing with their employer.

**MH** So if I came to the College to learn a specific skill, would you encourage me sign up for other things as well?

**MD** I'd be saying to you look, let's assume this is a 'credit type' set up; you've done these 10 credits with your employer. If you'd consider these other 10 then it would actually give you a fuller qualification and a broader range of skills.

**MH** Who communicates that to the students?

**MD** Us.

**MH** When you say 'us' is it the Directors or the Marketing Department?

**MD** I think this is what we are all about to be honest. Our strategy has four very clear strands which are; attraction, learner experience, success and performance. Everything we do is focussing on those four strands. It's about getting learners in and giving them a great experience. And that experience, I suppose, is where we would be looking at where they want to go and what they want to do. It's not just the core qualification they are doing it's everything else around it.

**MH** How are you going to fund all of this in the future?

**MD** I think it's about looking at how we set our budgets and re-engineering how the College operates. For example, when we talk about giving laptops to everyone, people say, 'how can you afford that?' If you look at the funding per full-time learner, (which is between £3,000 and £6,000), a leased laptop costs £100 a year. It's peanuts in comparison! So it's about looking at how we spend our money and how we deliver.

**MH** What mistakes are you working on avoiding in the next few years?

**MD** I suppose that's more a strategic question about making sure the College is fit for purpose, that we don't go down a strategic approach which suddenly the Government might pull funding for or an unsustainable form of delivery. I suppose that's the key mistake you want to avoid making.

**MH** What are the ideal future teaching and support staff going to look like?

**MD** They are not going to 'look' any different I suppose!

**MH** I apologise, that's me being a 'visual' learner!

**MD** It's going to be much more about supporting the learner rather than teaching the learner. It will mean a shift in terms of how we deliver. There is a lot of work going on right now about how teenagers interact, how they use the web and social networking. The future teaching staff will know to bring some of that into the learning environment.

**MH** Are you starting to do that now and if so can you give me an example of that?

**MD** Just using the virtual learning environment a lot more and ensuring that all course work is on there. We have some practical things like every member of staff has a laptop, every room has an electronic whiteboard, and this is encouraging the use of technology. Then looking at different ways our students can be supported, such as online, but it's early days. Our focus is the new College which is three years away, it's about ensuring people have shifted their practice so when we move them into an environment which is very different, we are able to deliver from day one and have a very smooth transition.

**MH** What about support staff?

**MD** That comes I suppose to an element of the shared services agenda. The bottom line is we should be providing the highest quality customer service as we can to the student and to the other staff within the organisation. There are lots of things that in the corporate world are probably done more efficiently and effectively, so we are looking at some of those practices and bringing them in to the College.

**MH** Who do you see as your key future partners?

**MD** On the educational front obviously there are the schools, the university, employers and the local authority who become more important. When it comes to independent providers, I am a strong believer that there are some partnerships we can have which will strengthen the offering of the College. Then there's also the shared services agenda, we are talking to Tribal too, so this is really bringing in people who are the experts from different areas to enhance what we offer to our local population.

**MH** So what about your role as the future Principal, how are you future proofing yourself?

**MD** Well clearly it has to be in terms of understanding the agenda and keeping ahead of everything and understanding where things are going. I would like to think my role would be much more about co-ordinating and liaising with those partners – especially the employers. It's almost a sales role in some ways, ensuring that what we have to offer is out there. I don't think my job now or in the future is to actually run the operation of the College – I've got others that can do that very effectively and with the right systems in place I can easily monitor progress.

**MH** If I told you that you were going to be given a brand new college to be built from scratch, what would be the three things you would focus on first?

**MD** Flexible use of space. Develop a more '365 days a year' offer. With a new building and the expertise we have in colleges, there is no reason why we shouldn't be a trainer of first choice to all employers. I would focus on how we could position ourselves with that.

I think that to really 'future proof' the College we need to work a lot closer with other colleges because I also think the days of expanding funding and resources will disappear and it will get somewhat tighter. We could work a lot more effectively across organisations enhanced by web and new technologies.

*"The best way to predict the future is to invent it."*

*Alan Kay*

# 21

## RADAR Thinking™

# RADAR Thinking™

Here's an extract taken from my book *Five Star Service – One Star Budget* published by Pearson, Prentice Hall. As customer service becomes increasingly important to FE, this model gives you a simple way to turn recurring problems into opportunities to shine.

## RADAR Thinking™

What do you do if you have a common problem that comes up time after time? You know the customer isn't going to be happy but you can't do anything about it; it really is outside of your control.

Radar is a wonderful invention. It prevents catastrophes every day. It doesn't remove the hazard, it just tells you where it is and more importantly how to avoid it.

So RADAR Thinking takes situations where you previously thought you had a nightmare and turns them into customer service opportunities.

Use RADAR as an acronym;

Realise
Assess
Decide
Act
Review

**Realise** – That you actually have a problem. Get your head out of the sand and take a look at the regular challenges your customers face. Is it delivery times? Sub contractors? Costs? Your environment?

Once you have a list...

**Assess** – Have a really good brainstorm and throw lots of ideas into the pot. If you really are going to have a powerful brainstorm session make sure you use the 3 golden rules.

**1)** Write down every idea

**2)** Keep it positive (ban anyone who says 'we've tried that before and it didn't work' or 'no')

**3)** Allow everyone an opportunity to participate.

Once you have assessed all your ideas...

**Decide** – Which ideas you are going to use and which ones you are going to park (or bin) for another day. Take the very best ideas and make sure they compliment the real problem (go back to Realise and check).

Once you have one or two which you are committed to...

**Action** – Decisions without actions are pretty worthless. Have you heard the story of the 4 frogs sat on the log? 1 decided to jump off – how many frogs were left? The answer is 4 because the frog only decided to jump off, he didn't actually do it! Ensure you put your ideas into practice swiftly and that everyone knows what you are doing.

Once you have the ideas in place...

**Review** – Take time to fine tune or, if needs be, ditch an idea. Forget about that nonsense of 'get it right the first time', go for getting it right by doing it. There aren't many ideas that changed the world by needing to be right the first time. Authors' note; if you are a pilot or surgeon and reading this, the 'get it right the first time' DOES apply to you!

Once understood, you can use the RADAR technique as part of your weekly meetings or monthly staff training. The more people who are involved with the ownership of the ideas, the better it works.

## RADAR Thinking at work

Here are two examples of RADAR Thinking being used to turn a regular challenge into a wonderful customer service experience.

I guess no customer service experience would be complete without an example from Disney.

Epcot in Orlando, Florida is Disney's biggest park and as you would expect has a very large car park. If you have ever visited Epcot, and driven there, you'll know the scale is huge! The Epcot car park alone can take up to 20,000 cars!

Logistically to get everyone from their cars to the park at the start of the day or from the park to their cars at the end of the day is a huge task so it doesn't help when a weary family get to the end of a long day and tell a Disney 'cast member' (their name for 'staff') that they can't remember where they've parked their car. This would be a nuisance if it happened to a dozen or so families, but on busy days up to 500 people have lost their cars!

Conventional thinking would be to suggest to the customer how utterly thick they have been and suggest they wait until everyone else has gone home. Then one of the remaining cars in the 30 acre car park would be theirs – and you hope they've learned a valuable lesson!

It was suggested at one point that Disney could have a lost car waiting area where families could shelter, watch cartoons and purchase snacks. Then when the car park cleared, a special 'Find your car' train would leave with everyone frantically pressing their remote key-fobs until some lights flashed. Good fun and a nice idea but at the end of a long day what do you want? That's right – you just want your car back.

Here's how they fixed the problem allowing over 90% of people to find their car in less than five minutes.

When you are collected from the car park, a road train takes you from your row in the car park to the entrance. The train driver asks you to remember the name of your car park (all named after Disney characters) and the row you have parked in. He even gets you to say it out loud. But by the end of the day, some people are so excited (and exhausted) that their car park name and row number are just a distant memory.

So (and here's the Disney magic) the driver who picks you up also writes the exact time he or she arrived to collect you, the name of the car park and the row number. Then, should you lose your car, the cast member assigned to help you locate it will ask, 'do you remember what time you arrived?' In most cases people remember the time they arrived because they are: a) proud of the fact they got there early b) rushing because the gates have or are about to open c) thinking about how much of their day has been lost because they are arriving late (Disney tickets are expensive!) Then they look down the list for the time and reveal that you were parked in 'Pluto 15' and a wave of familiarity washes over you.

This simple, yet effective system, thrills customers, frees up valuable staff time and can be duplicated effortlessly.

My friend Nicola called me the other day and said, 'Dyson vacuum cleaners use RADAR'. I've never worked with them so I'm sure they don't call it RADAR Thinking but their idea was simple and effective.

Nicola's Dyson stopped working. After 3 years of trouble free vacuuming it just stopped. The first bit of RADAR Thinking was obvious when she found the help line number on the cleaner (because people don't keep manuals). Second was when she called the help line on a Saturday evening, someone responded to her call because 'people use Dyson's at all times, so we have to be here at all times', said the customer service agent. A quick diagnostic predicted a burned-out motor. An engineer would be sent out and it would cost a maximum of £50 no matter what the problem was.

The engineer arrived, on time and looking smart, and sure enough the problem was the motor which he replaced. And he changed the cable because that looked a little worn, and fitted a new plug, because the other one was cracked, and replaced the filter. Then finally 'smartened up' the whole machine (all for the agreed price of £50).

Then RADAR really kicked in as the engineer asked Nicola if she knew how to wash the filter or if she knew she was supposed to do it every six months. No and no was her response. It turns out that the number one reason a motor burns out is because users don't clean the filter and that it should be done every six months. So he showed Nicola how to take it out, how to wash it and how to replace it.

Then he asked if she had a PC and took her to the Dyson website. He registered a request for her to receive a six-monthly email reminding her to clean the filter, because 'we could be better at remembering stuff like that'.

One other thing, while she was on the site she was offered 10% off attachments and ended up buying another £60 worth of products!

Reproduced with permission © Pearson Prentice Hall 2006

*"I decided not to let my past rule my future so I decided to change my present in order to open up my future."*

**Dr. Ana M Guzman**

# 22

# Interview
# with Steven
# Davis
## Sainsbury's plc

## Interview with Steven Davis, Head of Retail Resourcing & Training, Sainsbury's plc

*Steven has been at Sainsbury's for over five years. During this time he has had both operational and field roles and the last 3 years as part of the Retail HR leadership team responsible for resourcing and training.*

**MH** What are your expectations from a learning provider now and how do you see that changing in the next five years?

**SD** In simple terms I would expect to ensure that there was complete alignment with the Leitch Review principles. Making sure that everything that was being done by providers was focussed on employers' needs. I think that the earlier we get to that point; the more likely we are to start achieving some of the targets that have been set for 2010.

**MH** What three things are you looking for when you partner with a college?

**SD** Obviously, I think the first thing would be ensuring that the training delivered within that college was of the right quality and that there was a real understanding of business needs, not just from an educational point of view, but the whole piece around the softer skills too. So that's; communication, engagement, basic planning and organisation and some of the simpler disciplines that help get people ready to establish themselves quickly, along with the learning in the workplace.

**MH** So you are looking for someone who is 'complete', rather than somebody who's got a piece of paper.

**SD** Yes – absolutely. Secondly, I think there needs to be much closer engagement with, in particular, some of the larger employers. If I think of myself, I think there are a lot of opportunities. We've 150,000 people in our organisation. There's a huge amount of opportunity which is missed with the colleges engaging with the local communities. I've been in this role for nearly three years. I've never had any FE college get in contact with me and ask how we can work in partnership – never, which I think is a real missed opportunity.

Thirdly, I think, it's around how colleges need to understand more what the shortages are in terms of possibly. A good example would be craft skills within the UK. So for example I know that we have within our retailing industry in food, a significant shortage of bakers. So I suppose it's them having a more commercial approach to identifying what the need is, then responding to that need and working with the employers so that there can be real mutual benefit.

**MH** Of course, a good way to do that would be to ask you

**SD** Yes or course and spend some time in our business.

**MH** Would you be open to the idea of placements?

**SD** Absolutely!

**MH** How do you know when a learner has been successful?

**SD** One is, when we do training we always have a 'test your knowledge' at the end of every training period or training session. That is not necessarily for people to feel that they're in a 'test' environment. It's to give them, and the people they are working with, some level of confidence that they've achieved the knowledge of the skill level. That can give some people a lot of confidence knowing that they have got to that level. Or, if I'm working with a dangerous piece of machinery for example, I feel confident that I'm going to be able to do that in a safe way.

The other ways are observations. We encourage as many observations as possible and that comes to life in a coaching way, so the people who are being coached and observed are being given feedback all the time so that we work on a continuous improvement culture.

**MH** How are you gauging best value when it comes to buying in training?

**SD** I will be very honest with you and this probably surprises a lot of people, we do 95% of our training in-house. The only training that we tend to use external providers for is First Aid or some of the specialist Health & Safety areas. The majority of our training is done in-house.

The reason we do that is our business is quite a complex business so we tend to use the specialists that we have, who really understand the business. And because the business is changing so fast – retailers have to move very quickly – it means we can have a finger on the pulse in terms of changing training materials, making sure the training is right up-to-date and it's meeting the current needs of the business.

**MH** Do you do any work with Further Education at the moment?

**SD** No we don't. I'm interested in the people who leave FE and come to us looking for work and how prepared they are.

My team are actively doing some work at the moment where we've introduced bakery apprentices. It's a first in the industry and I am looking at some unique ways that we can start to work with colleges on day release etc. so we can have better partnerships, where we can really benefit from their skills. I think there's a whole piece about people who have been through apprenticeships also working alongside and experiencing what it's like to be an apprentice in different companies, not just in Sainsbury's. We will be doing work with some colleges but we're just identifying those at the moment.

**MH** What mistakes do you think Further Education establishments make that you wish they didn't?

**SD** I think that the most challenging thing for me around the whole arena of skills and Further Education is the complexity of it. I've had to learn quite fast. I suppose a simple way I could explain it is that there's a huge amount of 'wiring' and complexity and actually I don't want to see that wiring, I don't want to see that complexity, I just want to understand what it looks like in a simple way. I want to know how I can work with Further Education (or skills) in order to support what Leitch is about – and we agree fully with the principles of that – but also how do we get what is right and fit for our business? If I was to try and explain how it all works in a simple way, I couldn't do that. If I can't do that, as Head of Resourcing & Training, what chance is there of getting every one of our stores in the country to understand it? These stores could probably do some really good and exciting things with FE colleges at a more local level, but it's unlikely that I'm going to be able to get that message across in an effective way.

**MH** If you were to set up a new college what three things would you focus on first?

**SD** The first thing I would focus on would be getting the offer right. And I would do that by making sure that I understood what the need was. I would look at the wider need from a larger agenda; from an economic point of view and then a local agenda – so what do the customers need? I would do that by spending time with the customers. I would get into businesses. That would help me decide what the offer was going to be so the products would speak for themselves.

The second would be that I would surround myself with great people. People who really had a great passion for their subject but were also very customer focussed and customer facing.

Then I would also make sure that I was active in my community. That's not necessarily around PR principles, that is, making sure that people really understand the benefit that you can bring working with them in partnership.

Also, if I'm allowed a fourth, there would be some visual measures for people around success. A good example of that would be that I would want to then follow through with learners, after they've gone back into the work-place, around how we can make it better for them and how we could make it better for the employer by maybe helping prepare them better for going into the work-place.

**MH** What would your ideal future teaching staff look like?

**SD** I would like to see, and I don't know enough about this so maybe it is out there, I'd like to see a lot more people who have, like myself, business experience. Maybe being given the opportunity to go out and be seconded for a few years as part of their development; but also so that they are able to articulate in a very real way what it's like to be in business.

*"I've never had any FE college get in contact with me and ask how we can work in partnership – never, which I think is a real missed opportunity."*

**Steven Davis, Sainsbury's plc**

# 23

## Future savvy quiz

# Future savvy quiz

Here's a fun quiz in the style of a glossy magazine. Simply answer the questions honestly then read your results.

## 1) When asked about the future of my work I feel...

a) in control – if it is to be it's up to me!

b) unsure it depends on so many things outside of my influence

c) terrified, why can't things slow down a little?

## 2) In the next ten years nano-technology will...

a) be one of the most exciting developments in my life

b) mean things will get smaller

c) what the heck is 'nano-technology'?

## 3) To prepare for future trends I currently...

a) study avidly, reading and exploring what is happening around the world

b) am open minded

c) panic, because I don't know what they are going to be

## 4) After reading the opinions of employers in this book, I think...

a) we need to take some massive action now to fulfil their needs

b) we're doing a pretty good job

c) they should lower their expectations a little

## 5 I believe the 'Googlisation' of the world...

a) shows knowledge is cheap and becoming cheaper

b) means it's easy to look things up

c) sounds like a disease – can you be vaccinated against it?

## 6) A futurist...

a) is anyone who believes they can effect the future by their actions today

b) is a person who has knowledge of how things might be in the future

c) a person with a beard who spends too much time thinking and not enough working

## 7) Our future funding will come from...

a) exciting global partnerships and creative use of our intellectual property

b) a range of Government and non Government sources

c) the Government – it's their role to provide our funding

## 8) My future employment will be...

a) a series of contracts with a wide range of clients giving them and me maximum values, flexibility and specialism

b) dependant on how well I do my job

c) much the same

## 9) The five year vision for my organisation is...

a) clearly understood by every member of the team

b) available for anyone who asks to see it

c) five years? You're kidding; we don't know what we're doing next week!

## 10) The future of Further Education means...

a) exciting times ahead, there's never been a better time to get in to Further Education

b) it's going to keep on changing whether I like it or not

c) more paperwork

### 11) Our future partnerships will be based on...

a) exciting collaborations where we genuinely work hard to understand our partner's needs and bespoke our actions to help them achieve their goals

b) a wide selection of choices for our partners

c) take it or leave it we can only do what we do, we don't have the time to make everything different

**Mostly A's** You're already equipped for the future of FE. Make it your mission to spread the word and help others.

**Mostly B's** You're not worried about the future but at the same time you don't believe you can have a major impact on the way it will be. Take a few of the statements listed against the A's and challenge your thinking.

**Mostly C's** You're not looking forward to the future much at all. Time to wake up and smell the coffee, it's happening whether you're part of it or not. My challenge for you is to leave your cynical side behind and get involved, you'll soon see the positive effects you can have.

*"When you make a mistake, don't look back at it long. Take the reason of the thing into your mind and then look forward. Mistakes are lessons of wisdom. The past cannot be changed. The future is yet in your power."*

**Hugh White**

# 24

# Interview with John Latham

## Cornwall College

# Interview with John Latham,
# Principal and CEO, Cornwall College

*John Latham is CEO and Principal of Cornwall College which has a turnover of c. £70m, employs c. 2700 staff and operates from 7 major sites. John began his career in the private sector as an underwriter, spent 5 years at the University of Manchester before moving to the University of Liverpool, culminating his career there as Chief Operating Officer.*

**MH** What are you doing right now to Future Proof your College?

**JL** Trying to think ahead in terms of what "demand-led" means to us and our customers.

**MH** Give me an example of that?

**JL** Thinking outside of the boundaries of a college entity and thinking more from the perspective of what learners are looking for. Progression and seamless boundaries between schools, college FE and HE, which means rethinking complicated partnerships – which is always fun!

We're thinking on a timeline of 3 years. It's something that I toyed with in my previous career and having dabbled in it I am completely convinced now that this is the way to go. We seem to be working in a political framework and an environment that's more conducive to that.

**MH** The obvious answer is going to be the students but more specifically; your most important customer in 5 years time, what will they look like, who will they be?

**JL** I don't think this is a cop out I think it's a genuine answer – in 5 years time the key customer for any college (including ours) will be individual learners and employers. I'd expect a degree overlap between those two clients because employment and progression to the workplace is a major motivating factor for many of our students.

**MH** And what do you think the employers will be looking for in 5 years?

**JL** Much more flexibility – and I mean flexibility both in terms of delivery and in terms of the academic framework. And I think in 5 years time they'll get it. Some of John Denham's recent announcements around accrediting employer training appear to be confirming that direction of travel.

**MH** You've obviously got some big plans. How are you going to fund these future plans?

**JL** I think there are things that are common to colleges that we'd be seeking to utilise as funding sources and there are things that are specific to Cornwall.

I don't feel anything other than positive about the way opportunities are shaping up for plans that have a spatial element and an associated capital cost. The LSC appears to have secured a good capital settlement out of the last CSR and whilst there's no guarantees for any college (least of all mine), there are clearly opportunities to secure decent levels of capital contributions from Government.

We're a mixed College so we have a big HE portfolio and the Cornwall specific stuff flows from HE and skills and the infrastructure for both sits with Convergence Funding. We're funding partners in a unique HE partnership – Combined Universities in Cornwall. We've benefited greatly from that relationship over the last 5 years. I'm hopeful that will continue.

On the revenue side that's tougher! Cuts in adult LSC funding is putting an additional squeeze on a market that's not yet felt the full impact of hiking up tuition fees. And of course the roll-out of a "demand-led" system and redistribution of LSC revenue regionally and nationally adds further perturbation. But we're confident we can flourish in that environment. We have scale, a broad portfolio, multi-sites and a growing FE 16-18, HE and WBL portfolio.

I am also very clear that I don't think we should deserve a foot in the door with public money unless we're prepared as a corporation to put our money where our mouth is and borrow. And if that borrowing is on the basis of the understanding of risk and return on investment then I don't see any problem with that.

**MH** What mistakes do you want to avoid making in the next few years?

**JL** That's a really tough one. The obvious one to think about for a college in our position would be to fall back into an old style zero sum competitive mode with schools, colleges and other universities and I would really like to avoid the mistakes and risks that come with being narrow and insular.

**MH** Is it more comfortable to be like that? So the mistake would be to stay inside of your comfort zone?

**JL** Definitely, yes – that's a really good way of putting it. There's so much deep sustained change running through our sector at the moment. There's a real challenge being thrown at leaders in FE – no question.

**MH** And how about your future teaching staff – what are they going to look like?

**JL** High-performing, results orientated and driven.

**MH** And support staff?

**JL** The same but from a broader range of backgrounds than perhaps has been the case to date. I think we can hire laterally into education and produce a lot of benefit for the organisation and again for learners.

**MH** So are you focussing on that at the moment?

**JL** Absolutely. If you're talking about people to head up corporate functions, why not look to other sectors (public or private) to add a different perspective to your College's senior team?

**MH** Obviously partnerships are very important and becoming more and more important. Who do you see as your future partners?

**JL** Employers. I'm really proud of the quality of our employer engagement and WBL. We're incredibly well thought of by our business customers and that's such a valuable asset.

But I see partnerships and other educational partners as absolutely critical to our success too. That's going to encompass schools, other FEC's and Universities, but I wouldn't preclude partnership with "for profit" skills providers either.

**MH** And what about your role – the future Principal. What do you need to change and work on?

**JL** I see my role as being one of leading the organisation; setting the tone for the organisation, particularly in setting the tone for the management in the organisation and for being its key external ambassador; locally, regionally and nationally. I don't see that changing in the next three to five years.

**MH** Are you consciously wanting to create that ambassadorial role and go out to promote yourself as the 'front end' of the College?

**JL** It would seem odd not to do that. I don't see it as either/or – internally or externally focussed. A Principal needs to be good at both in my view. Our College is big – it turns over £70m, has a very broad range of academic activity across the whole LSC piece plus a vibrant and growing HE provision – so HEFCE comes into play. We work with 1400 businesses and enjoy satisfaction rates with our business clients in the 90%'s. We're also a major employer and economic force in Cornwall. That represents a big challenge in terms of relationships to foster, partners to keep engaged and audiences to communicate with. So an external focus is a given for me – the national challenge Foster threw down on the Sector's management of its own reputation confirms that. But we employ c. 2,700 staff and have around 45,000 learners on our books in a year. And the rate of change our sector is being exposed to at the moment means the need to lead that change internally and to communicate with your own College colleagues and students is just so vital.

Balancing these two aspects isn't easy – but it's an absolute requirement for any Principal.

**MH** If I was to say you have a greenfield site for a brand new college, what three things would you focus on first?

**JL** Employer engagement first and the relevance of your educational offer to a career path and employability.

It would also be great to have a blank sheet of paper as an employer and to build up our own T&C's and systems of reward.

The third is, I would ensure that we gave our clients/our students as much fun as we could possibly give them. We have a focus on that now. One of my deputies leads on this. The student experience – which we define as everything in College life outside the classroom – is a big priority for us. Despite quite a few difficulties, I've committed significant funds to that this year and completely changed the structure for making sure the students have a voice and the ability to shape how we deploy that resource and spend it.

*"The rate of change our sector is being exposed to at the moment means the need to lead that change internally and to communicate with your own College colleagues and students is just so vital."*

**John Latham**

# 25

## RANT!

# Rant!

### Genuine mistake

As I'm writing this, my publishers have just sent 100 copies of the wrong book to my office. When my Office Manager asked how it happened she was told it was a 'genuine mistake'. Of course, all mistakes are 'genuine', what other type of mistakes are there? Fake ones?

In the near future, words like 'genuine mistake' will become less and less acceptable. How will you avoid them?

*"The future will be better tomorrow."*

*Dan Quayle*

# 26

## Interview with Glen Hiemstra
www.futurist.com

# Interview with Glen Hiemstra, www.futurist.com

*Glen Hiemstra is the founder and owner of Futurist.com. Glen has advised professional, business, and Governmental organisations for two decades. He is the author of* Turning the Future into Revenue: What Businesses and Individuals Need to Know to Shape Their Futures...

**MH** What does it mean to be a futurist?

**GH** It means to engage the human capacity we have to anticipate the future and to envision or dream the future and then use those future views to give you guidance on the kind of things you ought to be doing now, in the present.

**MH** Do you believe that anybody can do that?

**GH** Yes. Anybody can do that if you redefine being a futurist away from trying to make accurate predictions of the future – which is the most common view – to trying to understand the patterns which are shaping the future and the techniques for creating a vision of what you want in the future. The way I describe it is you create an image of the future that makes sense and you fold that image back on the present so you can see what you ought to be doing in the next year or two or three, so that you can future proof your college.

**MH** Reading different articles from your website www.futurist.com there tends to be certain patterns, no rules but definite patterns that people follow when practicing being 'a futurist'. Would you agree with that?

**GH** Yes. Interestingly I've worked several times with Higher Education institutions having come out of that world myself 20 years ago and I can work with whole institutions who will try to anticipate and create the future. The point I make to them is that if you look out further ahead than you usually do, that is 10 or 20 years rather than 3, 4, 5 or 6, the patterns actually become clearer rather than less clear. The specifics are unpredictable but the patterns are discernable and you can then make educated decisions based on the patterns that you see.

Here are two examples. One is the global population is getting older – everybody knows that – but if you look 3, 4 or 5 years hence you think, well yes, but it doesn't influence us yet. But if you look 10 or 20 years out, then you have to ask what does that mean for some of what we teach, in terms of how we prepare for a world in which a quarter of the population is aged. So that has to do with subject matter in schools, colleges and so on. Then it has to do with who's teaching – what's an appropriate age for retirement versus alternative work arrangements that allow older people to continue to work longer? The third is, how might it influence the nature of students themselves? For example, if it becomes the norm to work until one is about 70 years old rather than 10 – 15 years less than that depending on where you live, then, might we get an older set of people who want to come back, not for a traditional degree but for some kind of work life transition?

There's an advantage to doing something which on the surface seems not to make a lot of sense, particularly to the logical thinkers. You may get people, the ones who'll say, 'you can't really know what's going to happen 20 years from now so there's really no point wasting our time on that'. They think, let's just play in the next budgetary period. When you think further out you can begin to make policy adjustments now, or begin to prepare for the next few years, or just merely say, 'in the next five to ten years, we should learn about the following three things so that we're ready five to ten years from now when it becomes more urgent to actually be doing and creating something'.

**MH** And what do you think maybe one of those three things could be?

**GH** The second major pattern, besides ageing, is the increasing emphasis on advanced education for long term success, and that's globally. Thirty years ago the US had 30% of the world's college students. Today it's 14%. In my book I make the case that we're in *the knowledge value age* and if you look at the next 20 years and beyond, that seems quite clear. That means everything and everybody is increasingly judged and rewarded based on how much knowledge they have right now and their skill at acquiring new knowledge and applying it on a continuous basis.

So, a second pattern is just the urgency of keeping up with the rest of the world. In the UK, like here, it's keeping up with China, with India who are educating lots and lots of people in Math, Science, improving general literacy, etc. And they are quite intent, as a matter of national policy, in leap-frogging ahead of the traditional leaders in education. There's nothing wrong with that, especially if we are in massive competition, but if you don't just want to survive but flourish in this knowledge value economy, you've got to think hard about how to increase the number of people who receive a quality Higher Education, and then continuously upgrade the quality of that education.

The third major pattern which is having an impact on Higher Education is the technology revolution around information technology – what I would call the 'Googlisation' of the world.

That's having two impacts:

1) It becomes easier for individuals to acquire reasonably good information on their own and so the education institutions have to ask; if we defined our job as 'delivering information to people who can't get it anywhere else', then what value can we add? There are all kinds of value about sorting through that information for; what knowledge actually is and what is wisdom, and helping people to see patterns. So that's one implication of the information technology revolution.

2) The second impact which I have described to Higher Education institutions here in the US as a trend though to be honest I think it is more a 'preferred future' at this point is the following. At any given institution, we ought to create a system where the students in residence, whether they're living on campus or commuting there everyday, are actually getting maybe a third of their instruction somewhere else via the global network. That way you begin to form alliances and within your own faculty begin to create lots of good content for the global student population. You really start to leverage information technology so that students get a share of their learning at your institution and another share at institutions all over the world while they're in residence with you. That means developing new financial arrangements about who pays what and all that. That makes logical sense to me – as other countries in the world improve their Higher Education and as the communication systems get more and more robust until they're fully visual, fully three-dimensional in 10 or 20 years, then it would be silly to go to one place and say that I will only learn from the faculty who are here.

**MH** I think students, like my 14 year old daughter, are doing their own version of that now, even with things like Facebook.

**GH** Think of your daughter and all young people born since say 1982. The leading edge of them are just getting finished with their Higher Education, but then think of the younger half of that group who have been born since 1990, in other words, tomorrow's Higher Education students. They are the first generation to be 'digitally native' in that they grew up with the Web from day one. They approach everything differently. They think differently. Brain researchers might even argue that their brains are being wired differently because they're always in a state of multi-tasking, constantly connected to a global communication network and they're tomorrow's Further Education students. Then think about the staff at colleges – they are 'digital immigrants'. They might be comfortable with digital technology, even quite skilled (although you'll find a lot that are not) but for them they're thinking, 'this is the new way of doing things'. For the generation of students just about to walk in the door, it's old news; this is the way the world has always been; what you have at your college isn't even as good as what I have at home on Facebook.

**MH** What are the three things you would focus on if you were going to head up a brand new college?

**GH** Wow, that's a great question. Number one, I would try and make sure I had the best in terms of globally connected technology so that students, when they arrived, could see that we have at least as good as they have at home.

Number two, I would look for a very globally aware faculty, maybe even a globally diverse faculty if I could.

Number three, I would look around and try and establish relationships with other leading global Higher Education institutions – formal relationships and strategic partnerships. A way of thinking of, 'you're going to teach this, we're going to teach that. Here's how it's going to work. Our faculty will supervise learning groups here, you'll deliver the content; your faculty will organise learning groups on your campus and we will deliver the content here'.

I would say those three things would be at the top of the list.

**MH** What mistakes do you think people make at the moment when they start to think about the future?

**GH** I would say there's a paradox in the mistakes in that people expect some things to change too fast – faster than they will. They expect things to be completely different. Think about this, 67 of 74 of the world's oldest institutions are universities – that's from Dave Brown at Wake Forest University. Universities have gone through certainly centuries of change. They have an amazing ability to be stable. So even though things are changing, there is a reminder that there are a lot of things that don't change and we over-estimate how fast they're going to change.

The paradox is that there are certain things which are coming sooner but we tend to think of them as way off in the future – such as the ageing population, people think we're talking about the next century. No, we're talking about the next two decades where the major impacts are going to be felt. People still think of the impacts of global warming as being 2 or 3 generations out, the end of the century – but of course we're already starting to see impacts now.

The paradox is, it's very hard to get the timing right of course when you're trying to anticipate the future. Something will happen tomorrow that will surprise everybody and there's no way of knowing that it's coming. And other things that we think are going to happen tomorrow, won't happen in our lifetime. That's one mistake – overestimating how fast things change. Another is underestimating how fast things change and getting all that mixed up.

The second mistake that people make is to underestimate the degree to which our image of the future tells us what to do right now. If you want to change what you're doing right now, change your image of the future.

The third mistake we make is again a kind of paradox in that we have to remember and anticipate simultaneously in order to enhance the present. We have 3 human capacities in terms of time frames; we can remember the past, live in the present and anticipate the future. It often gets so busy in the present we don't do much of the remembering or anticipating. One trap is to not remember the past at all. The flip side is not to anticipate but simply to assume that tomorrow is going to be just like yesterday, when there are a lot of signs that some of the changes are discontinuous – they're not just a repetition of old patterns. Again, it's hard to discern what all those are but if we go to ageing again – it's often called the 'discontinuous change'. It's just it's never existed in quite this way before. Or think about globalisation – we've had a global economy for centuries but what we haven't had is the instantaneous global communication that we have now, and that's new – particularly the internet part of it – that's really just 15 years old.

**MH** If there was any question that you wished I'd asked you today, what would it be?

**GH** Will students still sit in classrooms? This is one where we might overestimate the change that will take place in the future. The answer is; I think yes, more than we might think they will. The job of the faculty member – this has been coming for a long time – will be much less about transmitting content and much more about sequencing learning activities, monitoring learning groups, forming learning groups, helping discern what's valuable and what's not and so on. I still see lots of people gathering in small learning groups and it will probably happen in classrooms because classrooms keep us warm and dry. So in some ways it'll feel like an old classroom but because of the accessed information, it won't be exactly like the old lecture hall.

*"If you want to change what you're doing today, change your image of the future."*

### Glen Hiemstra – founder Futurist.com

# 27

## Interview
### with Joe McGrath
### Toyota UK

# Interview with Joe McGrath, Management and Technical Skills Development Manager, Toyota UK

*Joe has worked in Toyota since August 1991 in a variety of development roles, for the first 6 years developing members in the Toyota Production System. Following that Joe has developed and implemented programmes for Managers in application of the core business philosophy; The Toyota Way.*

**MH** What are your expectations from a learning provider now and how might that change in the next five years.

**JMcG** Speaking generally rather than specifically, the key thing, for me from a learning provider is that our agenda is their agenda. So that they are interested in what we want and are truly listening to what we are saying rather than trying to flog things that they have that they think we should have.

**MH** And how do you see that changing in the next five years?

**JMcG** It will become even more important than it is now. The pace of change is increasing so there will be a need to do things quicker, a need to make sure that they respond to changing needs of business, they will just have to act much quicker, and be able to design programmes in half the time that they take currently.

**MH** What three things are you aiming for when you partner with a college?

**JMcG** We are looking for long term partnerships, so mutual benefit in terms of; it's good for the college and it's good for us. We are also looking for consistency of delivery, so we are looking for a partner that not only understands Toyota but builds and develops their understanding over time. And we are looking for a college that's keeping up to date.

**MH** How do you measure success for a learner?

**JMcG** Many different ways; there are pre-course and post course tests – we have all of those of course. Then there are appraisal reviews. We are looking at the degree to which the knowledge, understanding and skill that has been achieved is being transferred to the job – that's the real test.

**MH** So it's transference of skills rather than just having the knowledge?

**JMcG** Absolutely one of our big thinking ways at Toyota is we identify learning in five levels and the lowest level is **Knowledge**; in other words somebody has some knowledge for example in electronics.

Two is **Understanding** so they may know it but do they really understand it. There are all sorts of things you could know but have almost zero understanding of.

Three is **Skill**. Do they have the skills to be able to deliver (on the job) the things that they are actually knowledgeable in and have understanding of?

The fourth is do they have the **Will**? So they may know it, they may understand it, and they may be highly skilled but they don't care to implement it or they don't have the willingness to actually put it into practice. It's only at the fourth level that we start to see business benefit and the individual benefit.

The fifth is to **Coach**. They have used it so well that they have complete belief in it and now they become the next generation of coaches.

It certainly puts my job in a different perspective. Previously I would just think; give people knowledge and understanding and sometimes skill. Now I am thinking, 'what is the total system that delivers people who are willing to use their skills and ultimately become strong believers and coaches for the next generation'.

**MH** How do you gauge best value when it comes to buying training?

**JMcG** Certainly not on cost, cost is not an indication of value because we have looked at people who are very high cost and rubbish. And we've looked at people who are low cost and extremely good.

We have a philosophy called the 'Toyota Way' and one of the things that the Toyota Way tells us we should do is we should *go and see*. We design criteria by which we would judge a provider. So we will look at; their systems, their own development and how they deliver skills and will in members that they are training. So really, value is; can they deliver what we want them to deliver in the time we want them to deliver it?

**MH** What mistakes do Further Education make that you wish they didn't.

**JMcG** The biggest one, and has been for a long time, is that they try to sell to industry what they have got rather than think 'what does industry actually want?' I understand why they do it and that may be OK in a very static market-place, but things are changing so much that they need to get on industry's agenda. Things have been relatively static for a long time, but now it has changed and industry has to move very quickly just to maintain market share and competitiveness.

**MH** If you were going to set up a college now, what would be the three things that you would focus on first.

**JMcG** The first thing I would do is an analysis of all my potential customers. So I would want to understand what my customers want and I would do that in some depth so that I really understood; what do they want now; what are they likely to need in the next few years?

I would also concentrate on delivery methods, so that they were cutting edge because there has been a great deal of change in the methodology for delivering and a lot of colleges don't use it. They still have their own chalk and talk way.

**MH** So it is not necessarily just the technology, it's also new teaching styles and skills?

**JMcG** Exactly! I mean the whole language of influence in industry has changed over the last 10 years. I know we spend a lot of time and money and effort keeping our people up to date, and I am not sure the colleges do.

My third thing I would focus on would be the staff. Rather than have staff who were just wanting to 'coast' and look for a 9 to 5 which is 'just another job', I would look for people who were passionate and really wanted to be in the enterprise and had some energy about them.

**MH** That's really the answer to my last question, what do you think the ideal future teaching staff will be like?

**JMcG** I don't think it is anything to do with age, it's purely to do with; are they customer focused? Do they continuously want to develop themselves? Are they open to new technologies? Are they building high levels of rapport between themselves and students? In other words, have they taken their attitude and their teaching mentality into the 21st century? Are they looking to challenge themselves and recognise that they are going to need to learn as much as the people they are teaching?

**MH** Any question that you wish I had asked you?

**JMcG** I think that those are a pretty good set of questions.

One which is a little bit different from the ones you have been asking. I'll tell you what the problem is and then maybe you can tell me what the question is.

I think colleges tend to be very secretive with their funding mechanisms, they have got people who are experts in funding and probably that's all they do. They know how to get the last penny out of the latest Government funding pot. This secrecy about these sources can lead to a lack of mutual trust (something which is important in our business). I'd like colleges to be more open and transparent – so that we can take the working relationship to a higher level of understanding.

*"One of our big thinking ways at Toyota is we identify learning in five levels and the lowest level is knowledge."*

**Joe McGrath, Toyota UK**

# 28

# Interview with Fintan Donohue

## North Herts. College

# Interview with Fintan Donohue, Principal and Chief Executive, North Hertfordshire College

*Fintan Donohue is Principal & Chief Executive of North Hertfordshire College. He has worked extensively with both public and private organisations to improve performance and raise motivation. While at Barnfield College, Fintan led the development of 6 Centres of Vocational Excellence and has a reputation for innovation in the sector.*

**MH** What are you doing right now to Future Proof your College?

**FD** We are making significant strategic investment in the actual resources and facilities of the organisation for the future. So to that extent we are making a £50m investment in two new academies, which are very much about looking at where employment in creative industries, sports and health might be in 2012 – 2015. One element is obviously major investment in the building infrastructure with an eye on the future. We are radically altering the curriculum offer with a focus upon what skills will be needed in the future. We are having to reposition the College completely for five years hence. Policy is being shaped by the Leitch Agenda but it also needs to be driven by what the changing needs of industry are going to look like.

It's not just about being driven by Leitch; it's actually recognising that the Principal's role is to understand where the College needs to be five years on in a knowledge economy. Increasingly the learners, who at one time would have entered our College looking for what I might call level 1/2 skills, now need to be taken to a level 3/4 outcome. We need to really look for a leading edge curriculum, which is where industry really wants us to be. So that's about changing our whole curriculum offer. In real terms for example, we have shifted £1m worth of curriculum in this year alone from what I would call generic provision into more skills based provision.

**MH** That huge isn't it?

**FD** It is huge but that's the scale of the challenge involved in preparing for a new future, which has changed the College's direction and mission. Our mission is now more about employability in terms of our community and less about the delivery of general provision in adult environments.

Alongside this is the changing skills base of our workforce. We have lost about 30 staff through voluntary and related redundancy in the last 18 months. We have had to bring in (for the first time to our College) new training courses like construction skills, so we are shifting the profile of our workforce to have a workforce that is more geared up for the future.

**MH** Who do you think your most important customer is going to be in five years time?

**FD** If your most important customer is where your dependency is in terms of funding – so that you are able to deliver what you want to deliver – then inevitably, in the future it's the relationship with the Local Authority. It becomes quite strategically significant that Local Authorities become more involved in the FE sector. There's a shift in that they will be a major purchaser in future. Our dependency on that funding I hope will be less but will still account for a very significant proportion of our full-time funding base and therefore become a very strategically significant customer in terms of supporting our vision on moving forward.

**MH** So do you see yourself as a key influencer for them now to support what you need to have in place for the five or ten year plan......?

**FD** Definitely. The time is now, and they have been very supportive with us for example in building a new engineering infrastructure skills base in Stevenage. We have engaged fully with them in terms of supporting our strategy for NEETS and curriculum that will address the needs of young people. With the Building Schools for the Future agenda (which is quite significant in my area) the Local Authority is currently engaged in re-building schools on the Government agenda. If they re-build those schools in a way which actually either duplicates or doesn't complement our vocational vision for the future now, then that could be hugely wasteful and very problematic in terms of economies of scale in the future. So it is really fundamental that we are together now planning – not just obviously the College's provision for the future – but really how the whole school's infrastructure will mix with us. I don't think that's been as well understood as it needs to be. For example, with Stevenage, one of my major centres, I've got the re-development of five schools being re-built in Stevenage itself at a cost of about £150m and what goes into those schools is critical to the College in terms of how it looks for progression in the future and what sort of skills mix we offer. So yes, now is the time because those foundations are literally being laid as we speak.

**MH** How do you fund all of these things?

**FD** We have looked at it in a number of ways. Strategically we have gone for a large scale partnering agreement with a plc. This has served our short-term needs very well but it is not without risk, which has had to be carefully managed. Seek out strategic partners moving forward. Then there may be people who can actually deliver our vision more cost-effectively than we can, so I'm not 'wedded' to the idea that we have to move exclusively towards direct employment.

We can look at forming strategic relationships, which can help us to deliver our overall mission, even if that means somebody else is delivering part of it for us.

My three main focuses for the future would be: innovation, growth and efficiency.

Innovation particularly because I think that if you don't learn from the leading edge international experience, if you're not engaged with developments in USA; with the Chinese; with all of those developing areas, if you're not looking at new developments, I think you won't have what your customers are going to need and that's going to affect your overall funding.

I'm particularly mindful of the fact that technology should enable us to be more efficient. By that I mean doing more in different delivery patterns so that we are actually delivering sometimes larger provision, more provision off site, much more online. We're looking at ways in which we can drive up the overall student/ staff ratio and the general efficiency of the organisation. That's where so far we have got most of the economic and financial gain. So I suppose innovation, growth and efficiency are at the heart of a strategy that funds us going forward.

**MH** What mistakes do you want to avoid making?

**FD** To make sure that I'm thinking in the future rather than the present. That is my main strand. I don't want to make the mistake of looking at things as they are rather than actually looking at things as they're going to need to be; the staffing, the quality, the facilities, all the things we need in place in five years time

**MH** Tell me about your ideal future teaching staff – what do they look like?

**FD** I think they are a staff who continue to care deeply about learning and learners so what hasn't changed for me is the fact I still need a workforce that is passionate and interested in a vocational sense, in terms of actually doing something that can bring value and worth to individuals and society.

So, the first thing is that they continue to have at their core, not necessarily a commercial drive (which will be part and parcel of the future) but are passionate about learning and about actually helping people to achieve their learning, education and employment goals. I think the future teaching staff are more flexible and they are 'case-loaded' in a way that they take responsibility for groups of learners but they continue to have, in many cases, very specialist skills.

That fits with my overall organisation model which is that specialism will be an absolute key element in terms of meeting the post-Leitch environment agenda. Staff who will actually be able to provide for industry; leading edge, new skills so that we continue to have quite a specialist provision.

**MH** And what about the support staff?

**FD** I would like to have got to the stage where support staff would be more involved in College decision making. Not just more involved in contributing but would actually feel a greater sense of the value they're adding to the organisation. I believe their contribution is very significant but is still in some cases relatively invisible to some of the more senior management. They would connect much more strongly with their contribution to learner achievement. In 'Maslow' terms they would recognise the contribution in removing barriers to learning by creating environments where people can learn.

**MH** You've talked to me about partnerships already but who would you love to have as a future partner?

**FD** The partnership has obviously got to be with the industries that we most significantly support. So I'm already quite engaged with the Sector Skills Councils in a number of areas. They are not quite partnerships in the sense you might mean it but I've got to be engaged I think with the leaders of skills in industry. So I want them as partners. That might be partners in the sense that they're partnering with us as a sector because it may not be possible to partner with them individually due to size or scale – so partnering with lead industry specialists and organisations that can move us forward.

Partnering with the Local Authority stakeholders and continuing to partner with those who have the community interests at heart is key. So it is an extension of what we currently do but probably with a stronger focus on (what I would call) industry and those who are actually investing in the skills of the workforce financially.

Making bigger connections with the CBI and with those who represent industry. I'd like to be more at the core of their strategy for local and economic success. That would be a key element in our way of moving forward.

**MH** And what about the role of the future Principal?

**FD** I think we continue to be inherently strategic, so that I need to be a strategic leader who can build confidence in the stakeholders and the workforce – but most importantly, I need to be a leader who can deliver high quality outputs.

I think increasingly that as the next five years unfold, it will become easier to identify Principals as strategic leaders who deliver really outstanding outcomes. My own prediction would be that eventually Boards and others will begin to recruit those people who can demonstrate a track record in having done just that. I think that's going to be really quite fundamental.

I think those leaders are becoming more recognisable in the sector and therefore I can see a situation where really the Principals/Chief Executives will need to have stronger evidence of the differences they've made and hopefully their recruitment will be much more significantly focussed in terms of that end of the operation.

**MH** If you had a greenfield site and you were going to create a new college, what would be the three things you would focus on first?

**FD** First and foremost I would look at the nature of our business going forward. I would want to know what business was in that community. I would want to make absolutely certain that I understood where the supply and demand was likely to come from. Was I, for example, in a high density industrial environment or was I in a more rural environment? So how would I configure the business in the College to make sure I was meeting the needs of the community I served? I would really want to understand my environment in terms of; who I was serving, where are they, what are they and how does my new College connect with them. I think that's fundamental.

I would want to look at the capacity that I would have to build, the curriculum base that I needed to have – so if it's in the South of England, if it's in a high cost area and so on – how am I going to be able to recruit and develop a workforce that's going to have the capacity to deliver what I'm going to need in that College. Can I recruit good quality, expert staff and am I in the right environment to do so?

And thirdly, of course, I need to know that I can afford it. So I need to know that the College I develop is the College that the funders, the individuals and others will want to pay for, either at full cost or through a funding model.

**MH** Do you have any final comments?

**FD** You say that I have a wonderful College – I don't actually have one yet. I left a College which was probably number one in the UK to take up a completely new challenge for me which is the Principal/CEO job.

What struck me most strongly was that the real issue for me is helping people to understand what excellence looks like – I think that is the core. In terms of our discussion, what's really struck home to me with the College which is now moving forward from what I think was a relatively flat middle type of success rate profile, is beginning to move forward with an energy and excitement. We're going to take some time to get them to the top end.

The one thing I do think in terms of the Principal of the future, it's about not compromising on standards and finding ways to help people because they don't always know whether what they're doing is excellent. They don't really know what very good looks like. And the biggest shock I got moving from one organisation into another was realising that some of the things that I saw as extremely average were not necessarily perceived by others in that light – so it is about not compromising on the fact that if you're going to deliver excellence for the students you've just got to make sure that people know what that looks like.

*"I know not what the future holds, but I know who holds the future."*

**Author Unknown**

# 29

# Interview with Clare Hannah

First UK Bus

# Interview with Clare Hannah, Director, First UK Bus, FirstGroup plc

*Clare is the Learning and Development Director, First UK Bus. During her 7 years with FirstGroup Plc she has been Head of Human Resources for First Great Western Trains Ltd and Regional Head of Human Resources for the UK Bus division in the South and Wales.*

**MH** What are your expectations from a learning provider now, and how can you see that changing in the next five years?

**CH** By learning provider, are we talking exclusively about FE colleges or learning providers generally?

**MH** Generally but if you want to answer it in two parts then that's fine.

**CH** It's probably going to be the same answer actually. The key thing that I look for in a learning provider is the partnership approach. I want flexibility, customer focus, being able to (where appropriate) contextualise their learning into our environment; to be able to provide opportunities for business-related projects as part of the training. For instance we have a learning provider who delivers a bespoke programme for us, that is actually mapped against the Level 2 NVQ in team leading. It's not a college it's a private provider, but as part of that programme design we've put in a business-related objective. That's a project where they have to identify a business-related issue and then apply their learning through the application of this business project.

**MH** Are they live issues?

**CH** Yes, very live.

**MH** Have you had some success where people have come up with solutions that perhaps you wouldn't have thought of yourselves?

**CH** Yes, because these are the people who are at the coal face, the supervisors. So there are lots of very simple projects, which have been implemented and have saved a lot of money. Often they are projects where no one has even had an opportunity to think about what a better solution might be.

**MH** In five years time would you see that type of partnership approach being the same or do you think it will have moved on to the next level?

**CH** It's going to develop even more, with employers accrediting their training on the National Qualification framework. I think we're going to need to have an even more flexible and proactive partnership approach with learning providers. They're also going to have to be more 'savvy' about advising companies how best to accredit their training. And the private provider is going to have to be more quality assurance focussed so there are properly measurable and evaluated learning outcomes rather than 'we can do a customer care course – here's a couple of happy sheets', then off they go with £800 in their pocket.

**MH** What do you think the three key things are that you look for when you partner with a college?

**CH** I'm just in the process of looking at partnering with a new college actually so this is very fresh. The first thing for me is about their quality assurance so I look at their OFSTED report – that's the first thing. Are they grade one or two? Full stop.

The second thing is their responsiveness to commercial timescales. Like when I say I want a contract by Wednesday, I want it by Wednesday. I don't want it the week after – that's about their whole speed of delivery.

The third thing would be about flexibility, particularly with the whole

Train to Gain initiative. I would be looking for a quality college who are innovative in their approach. So for instance, we have lots of learning centres in our business, and to have satellite college sites actually in our business through the learning centres that may be supported by full or part-time tutors – that's the sort of innovation I'm looking for.

So it's; quality, commercial responsiveness and innovation.

**MH** How would you measure the success of a learner?

**CH** Qualification almost certainly. The first thing, which is one of our strategic principles, is that wherever possible our development (at all levels of the business) is linked to academic, professional or vocational qualifications. So we have thousands and thousands of people with qualifications – from a Diploma in Company Direction with the IoD to an NVQ level 2 in Cleaning, and all points in between.

**MH** How do you know that you are getting best value when it comes to buying training for First UK Bus?

**CH** I'm a bloody hard negotiator! For me, some of it is about cost but it's not all about cost. It's about relationships – if I ask someone to submit proposals for ten different pieces of work I expect them to be professional and well written. Then when it comes to presentation, I can normally tell if these are the sort of people I want to work with or not, and I can do that very, very quickly. If they are talking to me about things like; pre meetings, quality joining instructions, post course evaluations and coming to meet me afterwards, if they are talking about things like needing to come and do some interviews with people to see if we can contextualise the learning. That's the sort of thing which indicates quality and that's the best value. It's the combination of those two.

**MH** So it's definitely not just cheapest price – it's all about what you're going to get for your money?

**CH** Yes – I'm not interested in having poor quality, low cost providers. They have to be business focussed and commercial.

**MH** What mistakes do you think that Further Education makes that you wish they didn't?

**CH** I suppose one of them would be when I say Wednesday, I mean Wednesday – don't assume I mean next Wednesday. So the mistake is not taking the deadline seriously. The other thing is probably wrapped up with their funding stream. Some of our experience with colleges has been understandably driven by their annual targets for their Train to Gain contract. When we have people working with us in the business, we have a little satellite centre – if we can't get 12 people on a Thursday afternoon at 3.30pm in a room, they pull the course. I understand that it's because of the funding and they have to have bums on seats. But actually for me partnership is for the long-term and sometimes you have to take the rough with the smooth. That's about innovation as well. It's about doing things differently. It's not just expecting that a college can come into the workplace and provide the same model that they do for full-time students.

**MH** I'm going to give you a new job. You're going to be given your own college. What are the three things you would focus on first in setting up your own college?

**CH** Making sure that my Executive Management team was commercial and had business experience. Making sure my Heads of Faculties had commercial and professional experience.

Making sure I had proper performance management systems in place to fire the bad and promote the good.

There are a lot of teachers that should not be educating our young people and adults, and there are some that are just fantastic and don't get the recognition.

My team's motto is, "If you're not working on the leading edge, you're taking up too much room".

**MH** Do you have that on a poster?

**CH** It's in a frame! My team are all on the leading edge, don't you worry, and that's how I run my training and development team.

**MH** What would the ideal future training and teaching staff be like from a college perspective?

**CH** They would have worked within a commercial environment, not necessarily full time but they should have done some. As part of their CPD they should go back into commerce for short secondment on a regular basis.

I would be expecting them to work with a leading edge pedagogical model – so making sure that it is very adult-centred, it's very work-focussed, it's very appropriate to the learners. I'd want very high energy, very interactive and obviously qualified staff.

**MH** Are there any questions that you wish I'd asked you today?

**CH** I suppose one question is, 'What is our strategic approach to learning and development in the business and how did that influence our choice of partners?'

**MH** Ok, that's your question.

**CH** We have three strategic principles for learning and development within First UK Bus. The first one is that every piece of learning that we deliver has to be related to SLAPP that's an acronym for; Safety, Lost mileage, Appearance of fleet, Punctuality and Profit.

The second principle is that everybody has to continuously learn from the top to the bottom and there is no exception.

The third principle is that wherever appropriate, learning is linked to a qualification outcome; professional, vocational or academic.

Another question I would have wanted you to ask me is, 'What is our approach to Management Development generally? The answer would be; our approach to development generally is that (based on the strategic principles that I mentioned) internally we have what we call learning and development ladders. What that means is there is a clear progression of learning and qualification from bus driver to Managing Director and all points in between. Going from NVQ level 2 up to Chartered Director status; passing through 3, 4 and 5 NVQ and MBA.

**MH** So it's very clear if you want a career with First UK Bus, exactly what you need to do, what you need to be qualified in and what needs to happen next, and you can see the next progression. Very few organisations have that.

**CH** Very few – which is why I've got the Government, Open University and the Institute of Directors singing our praises and why we're winning awards!

*"The future ain't what it used to be."*

*Yogi Berra*

# 30

# Have you ever been lost?

# Have you ever been lost?

Have you ever been lost, so lost that you have no idea where you are? After a while a little panic sets in but then suddenly there's a look of familiarity, perhaps its seeing a landmark, or when you were little your mum's coat. The relief feels so good it was almost worth getting lost to feel it.

Have you ever had food poisoning? When you feel so ill that 'answering the big white telephone' is your main activity for 24 hours. When you do feel well it's only then that you really appreciate your health – and it took being ill to help you appreciate it.

And have you ever misplaced a valuable item and found yourself in a major panic searching for it? Rushing around looking in the same places again and again? Retracing your last steps and getting annoyed with the people who ask, 'Where was the last place you had it'? (If you knew that you'd go back and find it!). Then you do find it! The joy! The excitement! The relief!

It's probably the case that we don't really appreciate what we have until we've lost it so perhaps now is a good time in this book stop for a moment and appreciate what you've got now. What's right? What's going well? Who are you really enjoying working with? What powerful impacts are you making today?

Ok, have you done it? Brilliant – then it's time to go back to the future!


*"The direction in which education starts a man will determine his future life."*

**Plato (427 BC – 347 BC)**

# 31

# Interview with Stephen Grix

with

Mid-Kent College

# Interview with Stephen Grix, Principal and Chief Executive, Mid Kent College

*Stephen left school at the age of 15 without any qualifications. He started working in 1971 as an apprentice bricklayer and attended Mid Kent College as a part time bricklaying student. He returned in 2005 as Principal and his posts in between include LEA Inspector, Head of Post-16 at OFSTED, Sixth Form College Principal and Director of Education.*

**MH** What are you doing right now to Future Proof your College?

**SG** We are running a very intensive Leadership training programme for our Senior Leadership team. It's quite an expensive Programme built around 360 degree appraisals. The 360 appraisal we felt was an important part of holding leaders to account. What we're trying to do is develop a great leadership team which is responsive and forward thinking. It's something that started about six months ago; we're just over half way through the Programme and we've had a really big push on Leadership as a core issue. We're going to roll out the training to the middle managers as well.

We've also done a lot of work on vision and values. We used Sir Bernard O'Connell, the former Principal of Runshaw College, to kick-start the process. We feel there is so much external change at present that if you're consistent about your vision and values you are better placed to withstand funding turbulence and uncertainty.

**MH** Who do you think your most important customers are going to be in five years?

**SG** I think it will be our students. It's always going to be our students. Some people say the LSC is your customer. I accept that you have to keep the LSC, and whoever replaces them happy, but in our relationships, our customers are always the students in the locality and particularly our 16 – 19 students. The question is whether or not they want to come to this College. There are some subtleties around that, we know we have got to have a good relationship with the Local Education Authority, because they will be funding us within 3 years and they will influence the way schools respond to us. We've got to keep close to our feeder schools but ultimately the bottom line is always going to be those young people.

Do they want to come to this College? Is this College offering them something they aspire to?

**MH** How will you fund your future plans? You've obviously got some big goals for the future?

**SG** I think you've always got to keep an eye on your costs and that has got to be a discipline. We are very rigorous about our costing and we recognise that we need to diversify in terms of our income.

We're involved in a Public Private Partnership (PPP), which has the potential to increase our non-LSC income significantly. It's a 30 year contract and the contract negotiations are very lengthy and complex.

We're also looking elsewhere at how we can build relationships and alliances. A few years ago I think some colleges went all out for diversification without acknowledging the multiple risks. So, for us, it's diversification but with strong risk management.

**MH** What mistakes are you looking to avoid making in the next few years?

**SG** If you diversify too quickly you can experience multiple risks. We're doing a 'new build' costing around £80 million and we're borrowing 40% of our income. If you look through the financial statements of colleges now there are no more than five or so colleges which have borrowings at 40% of income. It's very easy to borrow the money. We've got to make sure that it is sustainable. A lot of companies have gone down because they've allowed their borrowings to be too high. I want to avoid overdoing it on the borrowing and risk.

I also want to avoid too heavily pursuing a single area. If you look at the policy change we have had in the past year, you see it can suddenly change your whole business. I want us to focus on those areas where there's the greatest dependency in funding. With the new diplomas coming in there's a real risk that they may not be as successful as people hope. There's a sort of in-built assumption that when they're launched, all of our students will desperately want to do them. In my view parents and young people are more cautious and we will need to work hard to market our offer.

**MH** How do you get that balance right? What's the secret?

**SG** The difficulty is that there is a lot of pressure on you from the Government and others to embrace the new diplomas because they're funding us. We've got to do it in a relatively modest way initially and we've got to do it damned well. We've got to make sure that we are clear about the progression routes and that the quality is good. Keep it small, put your best people on it and then really evaluate it before you roll it out on a larger scale.

**MH** What do you think the future teaching staff is going to look like?

**SG** I think the teaching staff that we want are people who have got enthusiasm, subject specialism and the ability to work as part of a team. Increasingly there is a real need for the curriculum to be personalised. You're not just 20 people on the same course. That conceptually requires people to think a bit differently. It's about being able to understand learners and respond to their individual need.

We will be looking for teachers who have that capacity, alongside the willingness to embrace change and respond to learning in that way.

**MH** You mentioned earlier about partnership with your new neighbours, but who else do you feel are your future partners?

**SG** Estate agents say that the most important things about a house are location, location and location. We're going to be co-located with three universities in what we call a 'multiversity'. I see the partnership with them as fundamental because we're working in an area where participation in Higher Education is low. It's characterised as; white, working class, low aspiration and low in terms of numbers going into HE. It's much easier to go into Higher Education if you've physically got three universities next door to you. There's also the opportunity to have shared back office costs.

The Local Authorities are going to be more important to us because they'll be funding 14-19 education. It's vital that they identify with us as their local College.

Employers – we've got to look at the relationship with some of the key major employers. One of the things that some of the most successful colleges have done is to build that relationship, particularly with some of their large employers. They see it as a joint venture, so companies sponsor some of their new building. For example, they sponsor the equipment so it's leading edge.

I can't see why we can't do the same sort of thing here. We hope to have that sort of relationship with the Ministry of Defence. The Police used to do all their own training, they don't anymore, they outsource it because it's less expensive and they still have the control. That's increasingly what the Ministry of Defence are going to do. At the moment, their training is very good but also very expensive.

**MH** What are you doing to force that agenda?

**SG** The fact that we're going through the PPP is forcing us to consider how we work and how we organise ourselves as a College.

At the moment we're called Mid-Kent College and the majority of staff are employed on contracts. If we take our 14-19 market we will want to employ people on pretty similar contracts to which they're employed now because they will largely be the teaching staff who will be serving that market. They will be doing a similar job as they're doing now, albeit with that greater move to personalisation.

As for the work we'll be doing for Train to Gain, and the external contract for the Ministry of Defence, I think we should be running that as a separate part of the College with different contractual arrangements and probably a greater push on performance-related pay.

**MH** There are multiple different things happening – the next question has to be, what's the role of the future Principal?

**SG** The future Principal has to bring to fruition relationships, and look over the horizon. They need to provide the leadership for that to happen at a strategic level, and create structure beneath, which enables the college to manage uncertainty and the level of risk that's there. Also to appoint the right people. To get the right people in place; give them the freedom to operate; to draw out ideas from the staff and to manage the financial framework within which that operates.

**MH** If you could open a brand new college now, what would be the three things that you would focus on first?

**SG** First of all think about the learning environment. Consider how the learning environment makes learners feel? You want a building that helps students to aspire.

Secondly, focus on the staff who are going to be there because the danger is you have a building that gives the right messages, with the right branding but if the staff are not working in line with that then that's going to be a major problem.

And last but not least you must get the curriculum right. It needs to reflect the local labour market and to integrate with the provision within local schools.

*"The empires of the future are the empires of the mind."*

**Sir Winston Churchill**

# 32

# Final words

# Final words

I remember when I was at school; over tea my parents would ask, 'What have you learned?' and I would rhyme off the day's wisdom. I've asked myself the same question with reference to this project and here's what I've learned:

You can't predict the future but you can prepare for it.

Technology is changing – everything.

You can't decide what your clients need.

Education is fast, but getting faster.

Most people over-estimate what will happen in the short term.

Everyone under-estimates what will happen in the long term.

We have a rapidly ageing population.

It's not enough to 'think out of the box' you've got to get out of it.

Knowledge is the lowest level of learning

Partnerships are currently in the third division.

Partnerships in the future will need to be Champion's league.

Don't tell your printer your book will only be 60 pages.

Think global act local is yesterday's model. Think and act globally now is the way.

Some Principals are so far ahead of others in their thinking it is shaping the future for everyone.

Don't rely on any funding stream.

You can go from being a bus driver to Managing Director via a structured 'learning ladder'.

Big companies want to do more with colleges.

The very best learners must be college staff.

One third of all the people who have ever lived to be over 65 years old are alive now. Think hard about that one.

The edges are blurry and becoming even more blurred.

Future learners will probably want to study highly specialist subjects perhaps on a Saturday night, via mobile technology, with peers from China.

Employers are demanding more from less and want it in half the time.

FE colleges can become the ultimate recruitment consultants.

A chap called Leitch wrote a report and everything changed.

Some 19 year olds want to 'give something back'.

People born after 1990 don't care if you have the latest technology, they expect it.

If you're not excited by massive change then FE is probably not for you.

### *That's a taste of what I've discovered, what about you?*

# Book Michael to speak at your next conference or event

Michael Heppell has been described as one of the top 10 speakers in the world. If you would like Michael to speak for your organisation at your next event please contact us on 08456 733 336 (international +44 1434 688 555) or visit www.michaelheppell.com

Michael specialises in the following presentations for Further Education:

**How to be Brilliant** – based on Michael's International Best Selling book and world renowned course, find out what you need to do to achieve brilliance as your benchmark.

**How to be Brilliant for students** – the key messages from How to be Brilliant redesigned in a format for students.

**Five Star Service – One Star Budge**t – based on Michael's Best Selling book this is your chance to learn how the best customer service in the world can cost little or nothing.

**Future Proof Your College** – based on the research carried out for this book, Michael's latest presentation takes you on a rollercoaster ride to the future and back.

# www.michaelheppell.com

Visit www.michaelheppell.com

- Sign up for our free regular newsletter.

- Receive 90 days of Brilliance.

- Pick up some great offers in our online shop.

- Download audio programmes.

- Read our articles archive.

- Find out more about how Michael Heppell can help you.

# Thank you to...

An amazing team of people helped me to put this book together:

Christine Heppell, my co-author, business partner and soul-mate

Ruth Thomson, who has lead this project with amazing positivity and calm

Vanessa Thompson who managed to get everyone to say yes and has the unenviable task of managing me!

The contributors who all gave their time freely, openly and for no payment

Dame Ruth Silver, Lewisham College

Rosemary Du Rose, 02 Ltd

Andy Cole, Dollond & Aitchison

Brian Turtle, Belfast Metropolitan College

Jo O'Neill, Center Parcs

Jackie Fisher, Newcastle College

Gary Groom, Redcar & Cleveland College

Stephen Heppell www.heppell.net

Rob Baddock, Milton Keynes College

Peter Gilroy, Kent County Council

Mark Dawe, Oaklands College

Steven Davis, Sainsbury's plc

John Latham, Cornwall College

Glyn Hiemstra, www.Futurist.com

Joe McGrath, Toyota Motor Manufacturing (UK) Ltd

Mark Cahill, SigmaKalon UK & Ireland Ltd

Fintan Donohue, North Hertfordshire College

Clare Hannah, First UK Bus, FirstGroup plc

Stephen Grix, Mid Kent College

The many colleges who booked me to speak at staff conferences, training events and student motivation sessions.

The team at Edexcel, especially

Peter Miller

Linda Rockett, PA to Peter Miller

Trevor Luker

Lucy Mallard, PA to Trevor Luker

Photoula Kypri

Stevie Pattison-Dick

Raj Thakkar

The team at AoC especially

Des O'Hare

Ben Verinder

Everyone at Pearson/Prentice Hall

Ashford Open Learning
Ashford Colour Press

The Brilliant team at Michael Heppell especially Laura, Mike, Ali and Sheila